CONTEMPORARY ART

FROM CRESCENT MOON PUBLISHING

The Art of Andy Goldsworthy: Complete Works: Special Edition
by William Malpas

The Art of Andy Goldsworthy
by William Malpas

Andy Goldsworthy: Touching Nature
by William Malpas

Andy Goldsworthy In Close-Up
by William Malpas

Richard Long: The Art of Walking
by William Malpas

The Art of Richard Long: Complete Works: Special Edition
by William Malpas

Constantin Brancusi: Sculpting the Essence of Things
by James Pearson

Alison Wilding: The Embrace of Sculpture
by Susan Quinnell

Eric Gill: Nuptials of God
by Anthony Hoyland

*The Erotic Object: Sexuality in Sculpture
From Prehistory to the Present Day*
by Susan Quinnell

Minimal Art and Artists in the 1960s and After
by Laura Garrard

Land Art, Earthworks, Installations, Environments, Sculpture
by William Malpas

*Land Art: A Complete Guide to Landscape, Environmental,
Earthworks, Nature, Sculpture and Installation Art*
by William Malpas

Richard Long In Close-Up
by William Malpas

Land Art In Close-Up
by William Malpas

*Colourfield Painting: Minimal, Cool, Hard Edge, Serial
and Post-Painterly Abstract Art From the Sixties to the Present*
by Laura Garrard

Mark Rothko: The Art of Transcendence
by Julia Davis

Jasper Johns: Painting By Numbers
by L.M. Poole

Frank Stella: American Abstract Artist: Special Edition
by James Pearson

Maurice Sendak and the Art of Children's Book Illustration
by L.M. Poole

The Erotic Object In Close-Up: Sexuality in Sculpture
From Prehistory to the Present Day
By Susan Quinnell

Sacred Gardens: The Garden in Myth, Religion and Art
by Jeremy Mark Robinson

Sex in Art: Pornography and Pleasure in Painting and Sculpture
by Cassidy Hughes

Postwar Art
by George Knighton

VINCENT VAN GOGH

VINCENT VAN GOGH

Visionary Landscapes

Stuart Morris

CRESCENT MOON

CRESCENT MOON PUBLISHING
P.O. Box 393
Maidstone
Kent, ME14 5XU
United Kingdom

First published 1995. Second edition 2008.
© Stuart Morris 2008.

Printed and bound in Great Britain.
Set in Bookman 9 on 14pt.
Designed by Radiance Graphics.

British Library Cataloguing in Publication data

Morris, Stuart
Vincent van Gogh: Visionary Landscapes.
– (Painters Series)
I. Title II. Series

759.9492

ISBN 1-86171-185-9
ISBN-13 9781861711854

CONTENTS

NOTE

All works by Vincent van Gogh are housed at the Vincent van Gogh Foundation, Rijksmuseum Vincent van Gogh, Amsterdam, unless otherwise stated (denoted by 'A').

'O and 'Otterlo' refers to the Rijksmuseum Kröller-Müller, Otterlo.

'London' = the National Gallery, London.

'MOMA' = Museum of Modern Art (usually referring to the MOMA in New York).

All van Gogh's works cited in this study are oil on canvas, unless otherwise stated. Many of van Gogh's paintings are about 73 by 91 cm.

The letters of van Gogh are taken from the *Complete Letters* (Thames & Hudson 1958), using the numbers for each letter.

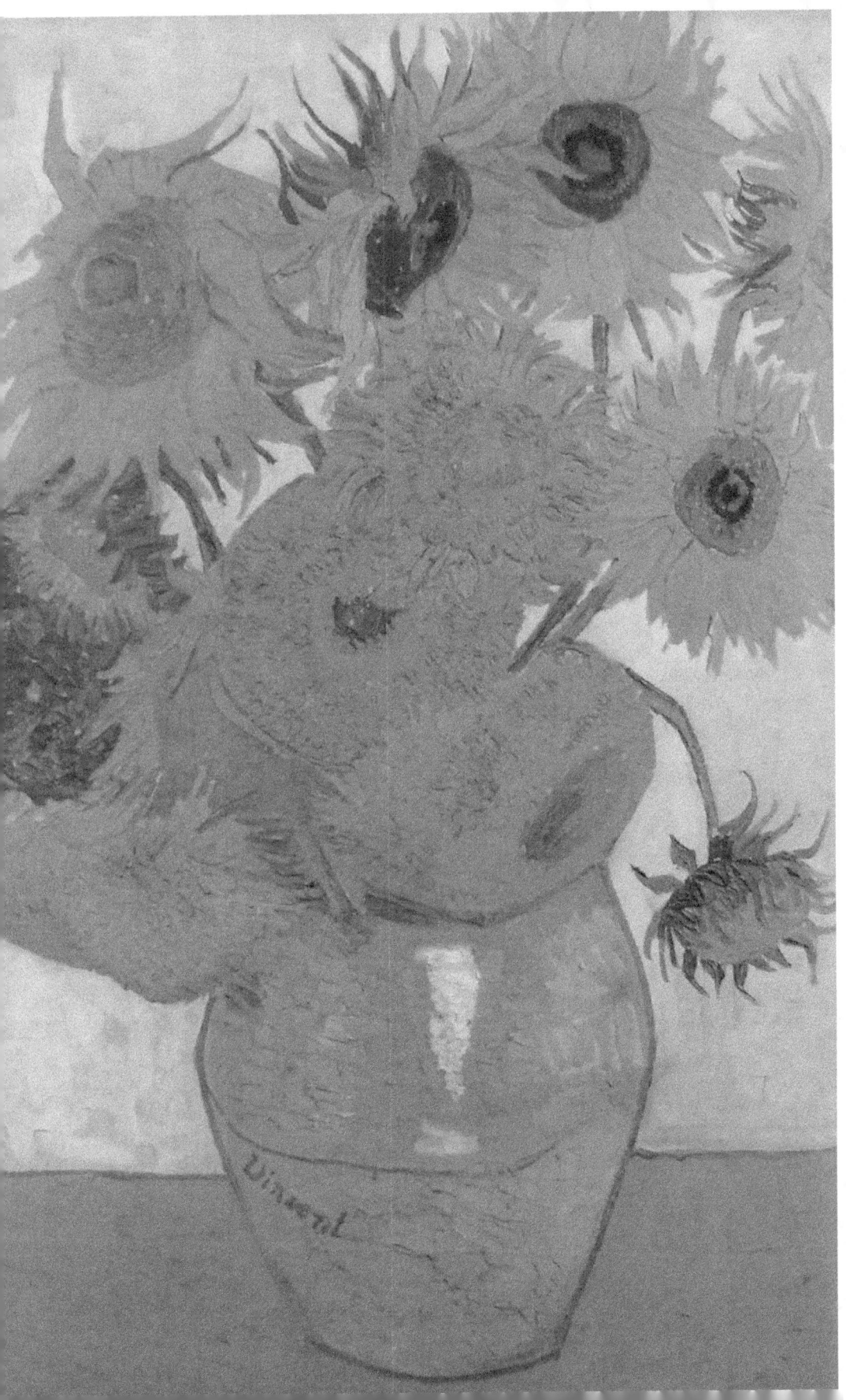

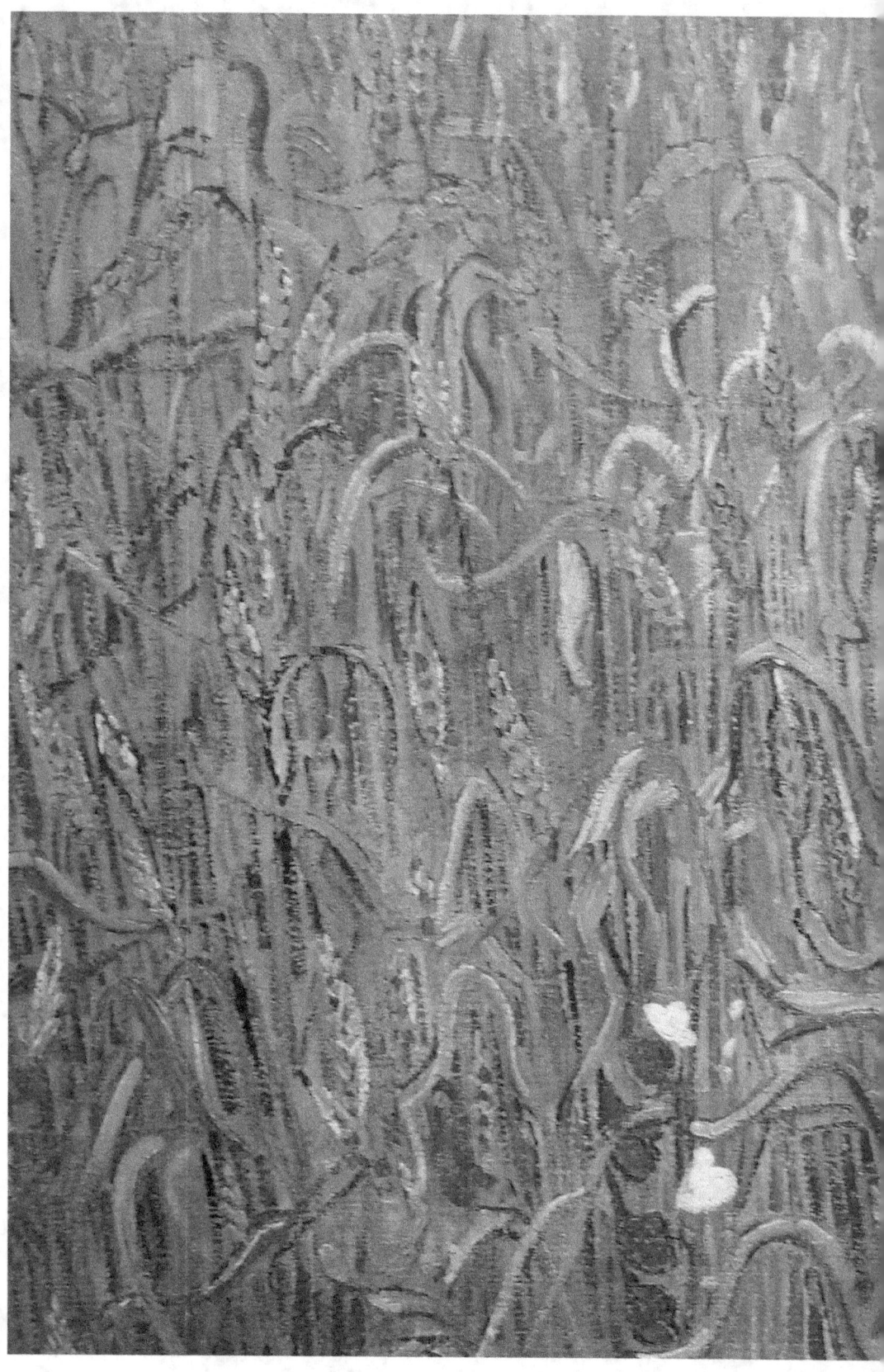

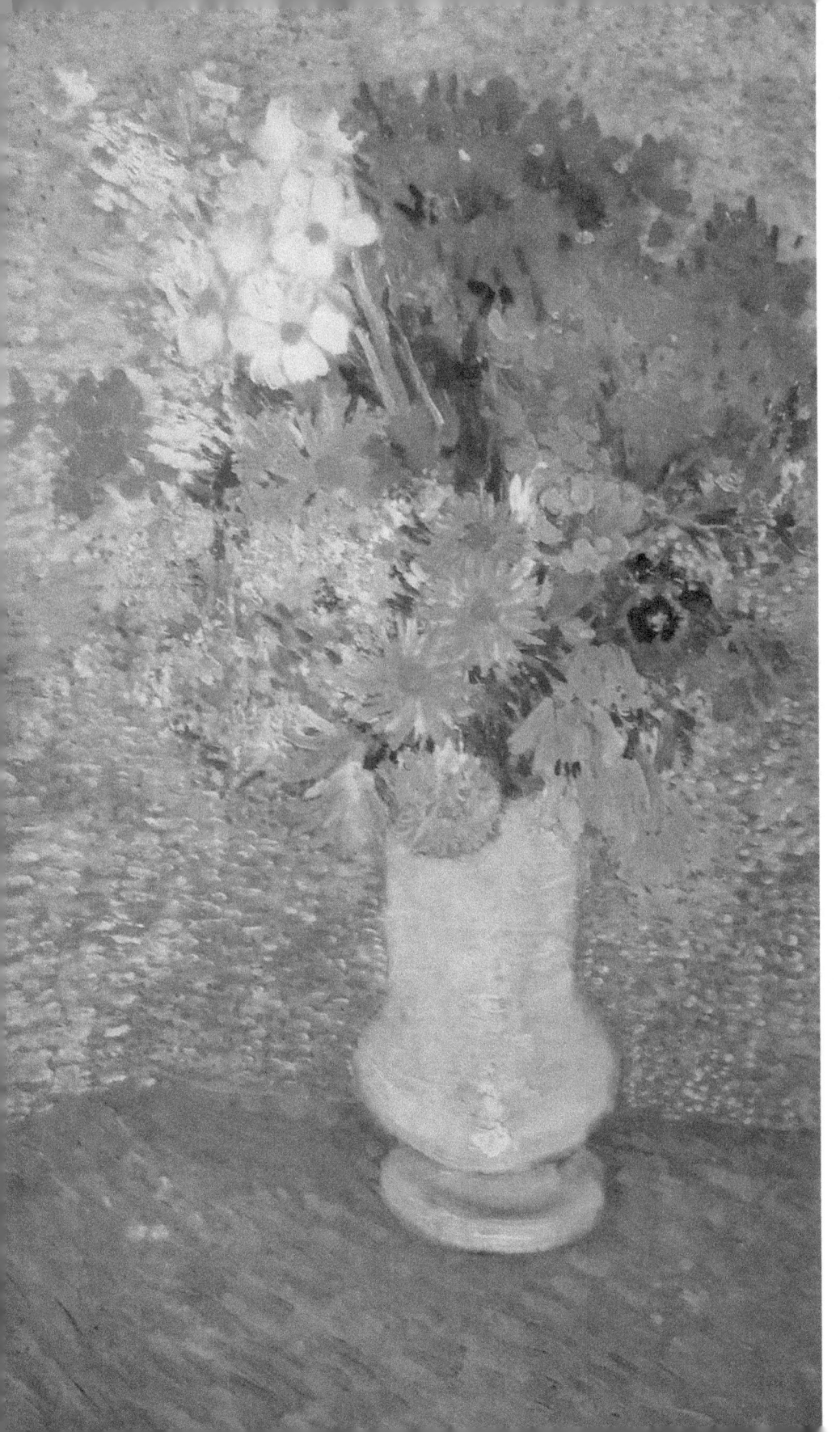

I

THE MYTH AND LEGEND OF VINCENT VAN GOGH

But if one analyzes from up close, one sees that the greatest and most energetic people of the century have always worked against the grain, and they have always worked out of personal initiative. Both in painting and in literature.

Vincent van Gogh, letter (no. 454)

Vincent van Gogh is one of the most celebrated of painters. Why? It's a bit of a mystery. The mystery (or irony) is that his paintings have commanded the highest prices in the auction rooms of the art world (88 million dollars, 53 million dollars, and so on), yet he only managed to sell one painting during his lifetime, and he died in poverty.[1] Why is van Gogh so popular? His legend has grown relatively rapidly. His art is loved by the critics and public alike. The crazy prices paid for single oil paintings are exaggerated manifestations of the fervour that van Gogh seems to generate. He is one of the handful of painters who cause great excitement when exhibitions of his work are put on. One thinks also of Monet, Leonardo, Michelangelo and Picasso. These are artists that the public go mad for, so that when they are exhibited, there are huge queues trailing around the block.

The 1990 centenary celebrations of 'poor Vincent' showed just how much he is exalted. There were films about him, discussions and conferences, TV documentaries, magazine articles, reviews, letters, and much merchandize was sold, to the great glee of the manufacturers: posters, tea towels, calendars, mugs, souvenirs of all kinds. What would the dishevelled, obsessive man who painted those small canvases in the years up to 1890 in South France make of the amazing fuss that now surrounds his work? What would van Gogh think of just *one* of his paintings being bought for 88 million dollars? It is a huge sum even in today's expensive world. You could build a hospital or two with that money. Imagine it! Did Vincent know that when he painted those irises on that small, standard-size canvas, that it would one day be 'worth' million of dollars?

> I shall count myself very happy if I can manage to work enough to earn my living, for it worries me a lot when I think that I have done so many pictures and drawings without ever selling one. (no. 591)

Most publishers in the 20th century seemed to have a van Gogh picture book out at some time or other (Penguin, Phaidon, Cassell, New York Graphic Society, Faber & Faber, Thames & Hudson, Weidenfeld & Nicolson, Benedikt Taschen, Harry N. Abrams). In these large format colour books a central group of the same pictures are reproduced time after time: these paintings form the centrepieces of the van Gogh *œuvre* and legend: *Portrait of Père Tanguy* (Athens), *The Starry Night* (MOMA, New York), *The Irises* (J. Paul Getty Museum), *The Church at Auvers* (Paris), *The Bridge of Langlois, Outdoor Café at Night* (O), *The Night Café* (Yale), *Van Gogh's Bedroom* (Louvre), *Van Gogh's Chair* (London), *Wheatfields* (Zurich), *Wheatfield with Crows* (A), *Portrait of Dr Gachet Seated* (Tokyo), *Sunflowers* (Munich) and various *Self-*

Portraits (Musée d'Orsay, London, Harvard). These are the paintings that are cited time and time again in the art history books, the paintings that are reprinted in books on Impressionism, or 19th century art, or the techniques of oils, the paintings that find their way onto teacloths and plates and posters. Many of van Gogh's *meisterwerks* are to be found in that van Gogh mecca, the Rijksmuseum Vincent van Gogh in Amsterdam (or in the Rijksmuseum Kröller-Müller, Otterlo).

The sheer number of biographies of van Gogh attests to his fascination: there are van Gogh biographies by, among others, J. Meier-Graefe, J. Havelaar, T. Duret, G. Coquiot, L. Piérard, F. Fels, C. Terrasse, J. Rewald, C. Nordenfalk, J. de Beucken, F. Elgar, F. Holmer, A. Parronchi, G. Schmidt, P. Gachet, P. Marois, M.E. Tralbaut, P. Lepohon, H. Perruchot, L. & E. Hanson, J. Leymarie, A.M. Hammacher, W. Weisbach, B. Welsh-Ovcharov and C. Bourniquel. There are studies, too, of van Gogh's 'madness' (by Schindeler, Cochrane, Riese, Duthuit, Doiteau, Rose, Kraus, Beer, Nigg, Bett, Aigrisse, Kaes, Gastaux, Mauron, etc). There are novels and stories about or featuring van Gogh: by M. Irwin, M. Elder, H. Kasack, C. Sternheim, W. Sauer, V. Drnak, S. Pollatschek, D. Burke, N. Stéphane, J. Poldermans, I. Stone, M. Geissler among others.

More of the later works than the early works by van Gogh will be discussed here. The preference is personal. However, I am interested in the van Gogh myth, and it is the later works that command the most critical attention.

Letters from Vincent van Gogh are taken from *The Complete Letters of Vincent van Gogh*, using the numbers in this edition.

Like the workers he depicted in numerous images, Vincent van Gogh himself worked very hard to improve his art. With a dogged determination van Gogh copied the Old Masters, as well as Japanese prints. His determined self-education and self-improvement paid off, resulting in more than 800 paintings in about 8 years. The years of van Gogh's art are relatively few – nearly all of the important works were made in the decade 1880-90. Hence his paintings are credited in art history books with the month and sometimes the day as well as the year of production. For most artists, 1889 would suffice. For van Gogh, the credit is *October* 1889. Producing 800 paintings in 8 years is an average of a hundred per year, or one every three and a half days. More likely, van Gogh have worked on a number at the same time, or within a short space of time. The price of fifty or eighty million dollars, then, is for a painting which had not had many hours expended on it compared to, say, a Renaissance altarpiece.

Vincent van Gogh created a series of paintings which have become a central part of Western culture (the sunflowers, bedroom, chair, wheatfields). These images are found in many places outside museums and art galleries. They have become populist images, like Michelangelo's *David* or Sistine Chapel, like the *Mona Lisa* or Monet's *Waterlilies*.

Monet is a key reference here, especially the Monet of the *Waterlilies*, in the Orangerie in Paris and at Giverny, the Monet of the Rouen cathedral facades and the golden haystacks paintings. This is the chocolate Monet, the painter of pretty rural scenes that flatter the bourgeoisie's sense of Nature and love of the 'country-side', a place for picnics and visits to country houses. Van Gogh does not fit so easily into this pastoral lovely-lovely view of painting. After all, van Gogh went *mad*, and spoke of the agony of art and the outside status of the artist. He was not a painter who flattered the tastes of the middle classes, as Monet did (and still does – Monet merchandise is among the most lucrative of modern artists). There is something disruptive and difficult about van Gogh, which partly has to do with the legend of his life, as well as the intensity of his art It is a difficulty and subversion which one finds also in Picasso, Rothko, Pollock and Modigliani, but not in, say, Monet, Bonnard or Matisse.

> What a queer thing the *touch* is, the stroke of the brush.
> In the open air, exposed to the wind, to the sun, to the curiosity
> of people, you work as you can, you fill your canvas anyhow.
> Then, however, you catch the real and essential – that is the
> most difficult. But when after a time you again take up this
> study and arrange your brush strokes in the direction of the
> objects – certainly it is more harmonious and pleasant to look
> at, and you add whatever you have of serenity and
> cheerfulness. (no. 605)

In his paintings, Vincent van Gogh's artistic eroticism is very
apparent: the sensual experience of putting oil paint onto canvas
is clear from very touch of the brush. This is surely one reason
why van Gogh's paintings command such a high price in the
international art world, and such high respect among art critics.
Van Gogh is an amazingly erotic painter. The pleasure of the
brushmark, the sensuality of rich impasto work combined with
rich colour is irresistible. As with painter such as Titian,
Rembrandt, Matisse and Jasper Johns, the thick application of oil
paint provides a hedonistic display of tactile sensuality. In
emphasizing the tragic aspect of van Gogh, as art critics can't
seem to help themselves from doing, they invariably emphasize
the sensuality of his work too. In the Nietzschean system, the
more tragic something is, the more sensual it becomes too. In van
Gogh this Nietzschean doctrine is very clearly played out: so that,
by the final paintings (*Wheatfield with Crows, Road with Man
Walking, Carriage, Cypress, Star and Crescent Moon, Landscape
in the Rain*) the sensuality reaches tragic proportions.

C.G. Jung's description of Friedrich Nietzsche in *Memories,
Dreams, Reflections* has affinities with the stereotypical
depictions of van Gogh in his creative madness:

> Nietzsche had lost the ground under his feet because he
> possessed nothing more than the inner world of his thoughts –
> which incidentally possessed him more than he it. He was

uprooted and hovered above the earth, and therefore he
succumbed to exaggeration and irreality. For me, such irreality
was the quintessence of horror, for I aimed, after, at *this* world
and *this* life. (214)

Jung seems to be describing the typical state of the creative
genius as a psychotic, a state of madness sometimes evoked in
descriptions of Leonardo da Vinci, Beethoven, and Rimbaud. The
Nietzschean tag is of course quite apposite for Vincent van Gogh.
Both espoused a fiery, masculinist, Northern European late 19th
century philosophy; both went mad; both had problematical lives;
both were misunderstood in their lifetimes; both were cultural
outsiders, intelligent and highly perceptive but unable to fit into
'normal' society; in both 'tragedy', theoretical or experiential, is
uppermost; both have been venerated to the skies by the
cognoscenti of the 20th century. One might say that van Gogh
paints the way Nietzsche writes – or thinks. In Nietzsche and van
Gogh the torment of subjective experience is radically and
lyrically played out. Nietzsche and van Gogh are the supreme
examples of the tortured, alienated, cultivated but misunderstood
modern European soul. The artist-philosopher as the living
embodiment of their work and principles. (Other angst-ridden
artists of this European outsider type of the same era included J.-
K. Huysmans, Arthur Rimbaud, Paul Verlaine, Knut Hamsun and
the doyen of them all, Dostoievsky.)

Henry Miller saw Vincent van Gogh as another of the tortured
souls of the late 19th century, along with Nietzsche, Strindberg
and Dostoievsky. 'And van Gogh! Why van Gogh is just a tortured
neurasthenic!' cried Miller in one of his essays on painting.[2] In
his book on Rimbaud, Miller wrote:

Of that band of martyrs, all of them filled with premonitions of
the future, the one who tragedy most closely approaches
Rimbaud's is van Gogh. Born a year ahead of Rimbaud he dies
by his own hand at almost the same age. Like Rimbaud, he too
had an adamant will, an almost superhuman courage, an

extraordinary energy and perseverance, all of which enabled him to fight against insuperable odds. But as with Rimbaud, the struggle exhausts him in the prime of life; he is laid low at the height of his powers.[3]

So many art critics seem eager to create the figure of Vincent van Gogh as a 'tormented' artist. So many readings of and books on van Gogh discuss the relation of his art to his life, continually relating this or that painting to this or that stage in his decline into madness. The common view is that van Gogh's art became increasingly tormented, like his life, ending up with the 'tragic' intensity of *Wheatfield with Crows* and the cypress and moon paintings. Was van Gogh this relentless 'tragic' and crazed, though? Citing the biography as an explication of (or inspiration for) the madness is too easy, and lessens the art and the life. There is rarely a book or study of van Gogh, however, that neglects to mention the madness and 'tragedy'. There was in fact nothing 'tragic' about van Gogh, in the Classic, theatrical sense. In the lyrical, Nietzschean sense, yes. But van Gogh's life in itself, like his art, is not innately 'tragic'. Intense, yes, vigorous and brash, yes, lyrical and sometimes crude in its bombast, yes. But 'tragic', no. Yet that word, 'tragic' is as affixed to van Gogh as is the word 'tormented artist'. One cannot unglue 'van Gogh' from 'tragic' or 'torment'.

The same overtaking of the art by the colourful incidents of the life has occurred with artists such as Beethoven, Rimbaud, Hemingway, Mozart, Modigliani, Shelley, Picasso and Dali. Discussing the way audiences misread Mark Rothko's colours, mistaking 'tragic' colours for radiant, upbeat colours, Harold Rosenberg said: 'yellows and greens that for him [van Gogh] were imbued were sinister drama have aroused pleasure in onlookers.' (1972) The idea that for van Gogh colours were 'tragic' has now taken hold and is rooted so deeply in van Gogh criticism that it cannot be extricated. But this relentlessly 'tragic' interpretation of the painter blinds criticism to other things that are going on in his art.

Vincent van Gogh is endlessly parodied: many people have made fun of him. He appears in many parodies, in pop songs, in sit coms, in magazines. Van Gogh's *The Potato Eaters* is embossed on solid gold medals, an obscene use of 'high art' for a low, commercial use, says Gwyneth Roberts, producing a 'mind-freezing effect... because of the obscenity of rendering an image of grinding poverty in gold'.[4] One can now 'own' a van Gogh quite easily, for a small sum: for photographic technology has progressed so far and so rapidly, that seamless fakes can be manufactured. Prints can be made onto canvas, so one can 'possess' a 'real' van Gogh.[5] At the same time, the prices that van Gogh's works command in the salesrooms of the art world are astonishing. It is the experience of the contemporary museum public to be humbled by such vast amounts of money, as Anthony Crabbe writes:

> A major collection like that of London's National Gallery is housed in over forty galleries, each fitted with dozens of works, any one of which is likely to be worth more than all the average visitor possesses. In a society that judges the personal status of the individual so much by their material worth, it is difficult not to be impressed by one's own relative 'worthlessness' in such an environment. Such feelings all too easily distract the visitor from critical consideration of the work with puzzling questions about the phenomenon of collecting, valuing and trading, and their relevance to the *æsthetic* value of the unique object. (in ib., 210-1)

It soon becomes apparent that Vincent van Gogh (or Leonardo or Turner or whoever) is expensive because of the opinions of other people, that is, a cultural elite. It is not the æsthetic qualities of the work itself that makes it so treasured, but the discourse around the work, the metadiscourse that is art history criticism. Van Gogh is one of the most obvious examples of an artist who cannot be viewed in isolation, separate from the huge van Gogh industry which has grown up around him. There is no van Gogh anymore, but 'van Gogh', a cultural commodity. Like Elvis Presley, who earns the Presley Estate sixteen million dollars a year or whatever it is, van Gogh earns a lot for other people, for buyers and sellers, for manufacturers who trade in van Gogh embossed items, for copyright holders and companies who sell franchises.

II

THE PSYCHOLOGY OF THE ARTIST

Your great canvas humming like a top.
But the terror for me is that you didn't realise
That love, even in inferior versions, is a kind
Of merciful self-repair. O Vincent you were blind.
Like some great effluent performer
Discharging whole rivers into hungry seas.

Lawrence Durrell, 'A Patch of Dust'[1]

Many artists have seen some sort of model in Vincent van Gogh;
seen him as some sort of a spiritual ancestor, or brother, a fellow
artist who embodied so many of the things the modern artist
experiences. The extreme emotions. The contradictions; the
veering from self-hate to exultation. The simplicity which could
become childishness. The selfishness which came out of the
determination and ambition to succeed. The stress that such a
driving ambition has on other people. The need for contact with
other artists coupled with the total dissatisfaction with them, and
with all people. The aching for recognition. The desperate need
for feedback. The constant doubt that one's work is utterly
worthless.

Again and again we return to the impact of van Gogh's letters. It is the fact that he wrote so much that partly accounts for his continuing popularity among critics and fans alike. His letters allow critics to follow every stage of his artistic career. We hear him moaning about artistic problems, or economic ones, and rejoicing over his successes. He ranges over subjects that include history, geography, politics, drawing, and personal relationships. He is loquacious and articulate, and this makes his letters enduring as well as entertaining. In a long letter of July 1880 (no. 133), for example, he goes on at length about his passions ('I am a man of passion') and makes metaphysical statements: 'I always think that the best way to know God is to love many things'). In autumn 1888 he says; 'If what one is doing looks out upon the infinite, and if one sees that one's work has it *raison d'être* and continuance in the future, then one works with more serenity.' (no. 538) In September 1880 he says he is 'in a rage of work' (no. 136), while on 12 November 1881 he writes that he feels 'energy – new, healthy energy in me'. On 9 April 1888 he speaks of being 'in a continual fever of work' (no. 474).

Van Gogh was a workaholic, no mistake about that ('*one cannot leave painting alone*' he wrote to his mother (no. 612)). The letters reveal a man obsessive about work, who lived and breathed painting every day. 'This week I have done absolutely nothing but paint and sleep and have my meals. That means sittings of twelve hours, of six hours and so on, and then a sleep of twelve hours at a stretch.' (no. 537) If he wasn't working, he was usually thinking about working or writing about working; if he was working, he was usually thinking about working better, quicker. 'Ideas for my work are coming to me in swarms, so that though I'm alone, I have no time to think or to feel, I go on painting like a steam engine. I think there will hardly ever be a standstill again.' (no. 535) His ideal was to keep working, whatever happened. He told himself to be content with small-scale, quiet, humble surroundings and means. Through steady, quiet work he might achieve something, he said in his letters. 'If I work on very quietly, the beautiful subjects will come of their own accord; really, above all, the great thing is to gather new vigour in reality' (B 21).

Van Gogh often groans about his own misery, much as other professional moaners have done (Woody Allen, Morrissey, Tony Hancock). He speaks of feeling 'an inexpressible melancholy inside' (6 July 1882, no. 212); in July 1890 he says he is still feeling 'very sad' (no. 206). Amateur (and professional) psychologists have a field day with personalities such as van Gogh. In his last letter (found on his body after his death) van Gogh wrote 'I am risking my life for it [my own work] and my reason has half foundered because of it' (no. 652). These words are seen as the ominous tones which precede shooting himself with a revolver on 27 July 1890. In another letter, of 19 September 1889, van Gogh wrote: 'when I am in the fields I am overwhelmed by a feeling of loneliness to such a horrible extent that I shy away from going out... Only when I stand a painting before my easel do I feel somewhat alive.' (W14)

Again and again Vincent van Gogh frets about the cost of living, the cost of painting – to body and soul, and to his brother, who provided much of van Gogh's income. 'It is hard, terribly hard,' van Gogh wrote to Theo, 'to keep on working when one does not sell, and when one literally has to pay for one's colour out of what would not be too much for eating, drinking and lodgings, however strictly calculated (December, 1885, no. 438) He clearly felt embarrassed and guilty about continually asking his brother for money, yet he kept doing it. He had to. He simply *had* to create. His letters abound in phrases such as 'I must' do this or that, or 'I must' have this or that.

> What a pity painting costs so much! This week I had fewer worries than the other week, so I let myself go. I shall have spent the 100-fr. note in a single week, but at the end of this week I'll have my four pictures, and even if I add the cost of all the paint I have used, the week will not have been sheer waste.

Vincent van Gogh

I have got up very early every day, I have had a good dinner and supper, and so I have been able to work hard and long without feeling myself weaken. But there, we live in days when there is no demand for what we are making, not only does it not sell, but as you see in Gauguin's case, when you want to borrow on the pictures, you can't get anything, even if it is a trifling sum and the work, important. And that is why we are the prey of every happening. And I am afraid that it will hardly change in our lifetime. but if we are preparing richer lives for the painters who will follow in our footstep, it will be something. But life is short, and shorter still, the number of years you feel bold enough to face everything. (no. 527)

Rainer Maria Rilke writes on van Gogh:

I believe I do feel what van Gogh must have felt at a certain juncture, and it is a strong and great feeling: that everything is yet to be done: everything. (22)

And again, Rilke maintained that Vincent van Gogh had a love for things which he did not need to show: it was in everything he did, not as demonstration, but as essence. 'He does not show it, he has it' (3 October 1907, 1988, 50).

...in his paintings (the *arbre fleuri*) poverty has already become rich: a great splendour from within. And that's how he sees everything: as a poor man; just compare his *parks*. These too are expressed with such quietness and simplicity, as if for poor people, so they can understand; without going into the extravagance that's in these trees; as if to do that would already be taking sides. He isn't on anyone's side, isn't on the side of the parks, and his love for all these things is directed at the nameless, and that's why he himself concealed it. He does not show it, he has it. And quickly takes it out of himself and puts it into the work, into the innermost and incessant part of the work: quickly: and no one has seen it! (20-21)

In the letters we see the intensity with which van Gogh ached for companionship, while at the same time fearing it. For months all he seemed to talk about was Gauguin – Gauguin coming down to Provence, him and Gauguin setting up an artists' colony to create the 'new art', he and Gauguin this and that. How hopeful van Gogh was that the arrival of Gauguin would amount to something extraordinary. Van Gogh's problem was the eternal one of the artist: wanting to share things with another artist, while being unable to work while the others were around. What Rilke says about van Gogh is pertinent here:

> I often think to myself what madness it would have been for van Gogh, and how destructive, if he had been forced to share the singularity of his vision with someone, to have someone join him in looking at his motifs before he had made his pictures of them, these existences that justify him with all their being, that vouch for him invoke his reality. (1988, 5-6)

That Vincent van Gogh wanted to be able to work, with enough to see him through, is obvious from his letters. However, there is also a deep desire in him to communicate with like minds. The sheer volume of his letters attests to his immense need for dialogue with other people. In his letters he craves attention, reassurance, inspiration, recognition. He wants to be appreciated, he wants his paintings to be seen.

On 15 October 1881 van Gogh states that 'Nature certainly is 'intangible', yet one must seize her, and with a strong hand'. He is always celebrating landscape – or, more correctly, his relationship with it: 'Sometimes I have such a longing to do landscape, just as I crave a long walk to refresh myself; and in all nature, for instance in trees, I see expression and soul, so to speak.' (November 1882, 242). Van Gogh's letters are peppered with such ecstatic descriptions of his communing with the natural world, such as this extract from a letter of Midsummer 1888:

> One night I went for walk by the sea along the empty shore. It was not gay, but neither was it sad – it was – beautiful. The deep blue sky was flecked with clouds of a blue deeper than the fundamental blue of intense cobalt, and other of a clearer blue, like the blue whiteness of the Milky Way. In the blue depths the stars were sparkling, greenish, yellow, white, pink,

more brilliant, more sparkingly gem-like than at home – even in Paris: opals, you might call them, emeralds, lapis lazuli, rubies, sapphires. The sea was very deep ultramarine – the shore a sort of violet and faint russet as I saw it, and on the dunes...some bushes Prussian blue. (no. 499)

In a letter of 3 September 1888 Vincent van Gogh expressed his desire to paint pictures that have the radiance of mediæval and Renaissance art. As he put it, he wanted to paint people so that they have 'something of the eternal which the halo used to symbolize'. The way to portray this radiance, in a secular world, which did not have the certainties of religion which the Middle Ages had, was to use 'the actual radiance and vibration of our colouring.' (no. 531)

III

THE ART OF VINCENT VAN GOGH

AESTHETICS

Paint has been laid on thickly for a long time – think of Bill Turner's late oils, or Vincent van Gogh in canvases such as the famous *Wheatfield with Crows* or *The Starry Night*. Certainly van Gogh's painterly surfaces, like those of, say, Matisse or Bonnard, are very erotic, with their feverish brushmarks laid on top of each other. Perhaps the eroticism of van Gogh's paintings plays a part in the fact that his works command higher prices than any other artist: $53.9 million for *Irises*, and 82.5 million dollars for *Portrait of Dr. Gachet*.[1]

Peter Fuller in a lecture on "British Romantic Landscape Painting" wrote:

> Clement Greenberg went further. 'There is' he wrote, 'nothing left in nature for plastic art to explore.' He even criticized Van Gogh for becoming 'too obsessed with the pattern glimpsed in nature'. Greenberg questioned whether the impact of Van Gogh's paintings had as much to do with art as with that emotion or quality of 'strikingness' which Kant distinguishes as analogous to the beautiful...[2]

Vincent van Gogh

Vincent van Gogh seems to show the viewer things as they 'really are'. Not so much the essence of the thing but the thing itself, in the Cézannean manner. Van Gogh, Rainer Maria Rilke says, shows the viewer a horse, a house, a tree.

> Or a garden, or a park, which is seen and shown with the same utter lack of prejudice or of pride; or, simply, things, a chair for instance, nothing but a chair, of the most ordinary kind: and yet, how much there is in all this that reminds one of the 'saints' he promised himself and resolved to paint at some much later time! (18)

Even philosophers such as Martin Heidegger were not averse to contemplating van Gogh's work. Heidegger wrote lyrically of van Gogh's painting of a pair of shoes (*Old Shoes*):

> From the dark opening of the worn insides of the shoes the toilsome tread of the worker stares forth. In the stiffly, rugged heaviness of the shoes there is the accumulated tenacity of her slow trudge through the far spreading and ever-uniform furrows of the field swept by a raw wind. On the leather lie the dampness and richness of the soil. Under the soles slides the loneliness of the field-path as evening falls. In the shoes vibrates the silent call of the earth.[3]

Heidegger's reading of the shoes became the subject of a discussion of another philosopher, Jacques Derrida.

COLOUR

Often it seems to me that night is even more richly coloured than day, coloured with the most intense violets, blues, And greens. If you look carefully, you will see that certain stars are lemon-coloured, others have pink, green, blue, or myosotis glints...'

Vincent van Gogh (in Lassaigne, 78)

...the painter of the future will be a colorist such as has never yet existed.

Vincent van Gogh (no. 482)

Seen close-up, Vincent van Gogh's paintings offer all the sensual pleasures one can expect from painting as a physical object and a cultural art form: subtle and brash colours, inner radiance, sense of harmony, balance, proportion, thick impasto and thin layering. Van Gogh makes the manufacture obvious to all – leaving the hessian canvas visible, leaving gaps around thick impasto, making each brushstroke as prominent as if it's been done in oil and wax. By painting likes this, van Gogh seems to leave a little of the painting unfinished: it then is left up to the spectator to finish off the painting. That is, as one considers paintings such as van Gogh's, where the edges are not smoothed out, there is a space for the involvement of the spectator in the manufacture of the painting. In other words, the viewer is invited to paint the painting, to follow each brushmark, to pull all the colours together and harmonize them, to add the final touches to the painting. The viewer becomes a painter: this is another reason, perhaps, for van Gogh's popularity. His paintings encircle the viewer with an embrace of painting about painting, painting as a creation and journey, with the viewer invited to explore, to touch, to follow the painter into each scumbled track of oil made by short stiff-haired paint brushes. Created in frenzies of activity, there seems to be some work still to be done in van Gogh's paintings. The viewer seems to be invited to take up the brush, and work on those thick surfaces of oil which still seem to be wet.

In the letters there are frequent requests to his brother Theo for money to buy colours. He typically lists his colour requirements thus:

3 tubes	zinc white
1 tube same size	cobalt
1 " "	ultramarine
4 " "	malachite green
1 " "	emerald green
1 " "	orange lead (no. 581)

As one would expect, Vincent van Gogh's tubes of paint are mainly landscape colours – greens especially, and blues. Indeed, in this list of paint tubes one can see a painting forming: greens and blues, with orange for the sun. Later requests to Theo for paint include 6 large tubes of zinc white, 2 tubes of emerald green, 2 tubes of cobalt, 2 small tubes of carmine, one of vermilion, and a large tube of crimson lake (no. 604).

From time to time there are moments when nature is superb, autumn effects glorious in colour, green skies contrasting with foliage in yellows, oranges, greens, earth in all the violet, heat-withered grass among which, however, the rains have given a last energy to certain plants, which again start putting forth little flowers of violet, pink, blue, yellow. (no. 610)

Julia Kristeva writes of colour in *Desire in Language*:

Colour can be defined... as being articulated on such a triple register within the domain of visual perceptions: an instinctual pressure linked to external visible objects; the same pressure causing the eroticizing of the body proper *via* visual perception and gesture; and the insertion of this pressure under the impact of censorship as a sign in a system of representation. (219)

Vincent van Gogh

For Kristeva, colour is a system of representation that allows the subject to escape from narrative:

> Thus, it is through colour – colours – that the subject escapes its alienation with a code (representational, ideological, symbolic, and so forth) that it, as conscious subject, accepts. Similarly, it is through colour that Western painting began to escape the constraint of narrative and perspective norm (as with Giotto) as well as representation itself (as with Cézanne, Matisse, Rothko, Mondrian). Matisse spells it in full: it is through colour – painting's fundamental "device," in the broad sense of "human language" – that revolutions in the plastic arts come about... The chromatic apparatus, like rhythm for language, thus involves a shattering of meaning and its subject into a scale of differences. These, however, are articulated within an area beyond meaning that holds meaning's surplus. Colour is not zero meaning; it is excess meaning through instinctual drive, that is, through death... As asserted and differentiating negativity, pictorial colour (which overlays the practice of a subject merely speaking in order to communicate) does not erase meaning; it maintains it through multiplication and shows that it is engendered as the meaning of a singular being. (ib., 221)

Van Gogh's sense of colour is absolutely immediate. It is a *psychological* sense of colour, but it is also naturalistic, firmly based in a close study of the world. Van Gogh did not create entirely in interiors; he was an artist of the open air, like Turner or Monet, and his colours are founded on natural colours. Yet, at the same time, Van Gogh's colours are wild, quite wild and strange. Even in mundane subjects, such as his chair, he produces strange colours, such as that sea green of the door to the right of the chair in *Vincent's Chair with His Pipe* (National Gallery, London). Van Gogh was always trying to break through to the extraordinary, to make the extraordinary ordinary, to bring out the fantastic in the mundane. Mircea Eliade writes in *Ordeal By Labyrinth*:

> I believe that the transhistorical is always there, concealed within the historical, the extraordinary within the ordinary.

Vincent van Gogh

Aldous Huxley wrote of the vision conferred by LSD as a *vision beatifica*: it enabled him to see forms and colors as Van Gogh saw his famous chair. It is beyond doubt that this gray reality, this everyday life of ours, is a camouflage for something else. (Eliade, 1984, 178)

This is the mystery of Vincent van Gogh, this tension between the imagined and the actual, between the psychological and the natural. The brilliant yellow and golden wheatfields in van Gogh's paintings, such as in *Wheatfield Behind Saint-Paul Hospital with a Reaper*, or *Noon: Rest from Work* or *Wheatfields with Reaper at Sunrise* are realistic, for fields can really be so luminous. Yet, at the same time, these bright golden fields have a psychological and symbolic significance, a resonance that some see as religious.

The imagination is certainly a faculty which we must develop, one which alone can lead us to the creation of a more exalting and consoling nature than the single brief glance at reality – which in our sight is ever changing, passing like a flash of lightning – can let us perceive. (B 3)

Van Gogh's colours partake of the late 19th century and Symbolist fascination with the occult as well as being quite naturalistic. One of van Gogh's more famous statements uses the psychology of colour: 'by intensifying *all* the colour one arrives once again at quietude and harmony.' (W 3) In a sense, this defines much of van Gogh's project in painting: an Orphic (mythic) descent and return, travelling through wildness (intensity) and back again, coming home (to calm). Van Gogh uses the basic tenet of magic – *as above, so below* – which comes from the Emerald Table of Hermes Trismegistus. Basically, the hermetic tenet says that everything on Earth reflects everything in Heaven. Or, more accurately and psychologically, that is, more in tune with our modern, psychoanalytical epoch, inner and outer are connected, even identical. Feminists couch this inner/ outer relation thus: the personal is political. The psychic/ emotional and inner realms are part of a continuum with the physical, 'objective' and public world. So the intimate, private orgasmic union of two lovers, for instance, is identical with the public, worldly energies of weather and Nature. This is fundamental to Western magic, this sense of unity in all things, so the stars can influence human lives (in astrology), or certain colours can influence certain acts, or certain herbs can help certain emotions to be produced, etc. The basic theory of magical correspondences, employed by Baudelaire in his poem 'Correspondances', occurs through Western art – in Shakespeare, in alchemy, Neoplatonism, and in Oriental mysticisms such as Taoism.

Vincent van Gogh's art is an art of correspondences. His art of correspondences, is part of that alternative to Western established religion, which includes areas of experience such as alchemy, tassomancy, astrology, cheiromancy, geomancy, Gnosticism, witchcraft, angelism, Rosicrucianism, Neoplatonism – all those cults, movements and beliefs which form the 'underbelly' of Western religion, which seem to be in opposition to Christianity, but which in fact fuse with Christianity at many points. These beliefs are 'occult' but normal – that is, they occur everywhere but are suppressed or hidden away.

In the key fictional work of the Symbolist era, Huysman's *A Rebours* (*Against Nature*), a decadent, dandyish æsthete experiments with various sensual stimuli. Arthur Rimbaud had written of the magic of colours in his extraordinary poetic sequence *A Season in Hell*. For Rimbaud, each vowel has a colour attached to it, each vowel has an alchemical significance.

This interconnectedness of colours and sounds or colours and letters stems from Charles Baudelaire, another precursor in sensual madness of van Gogh and Rimbaud. For Baudelaire, the world is a 'forest of symbols', where everything is linked to everything else. The link is the poet or artist, who sees the links and makes them clear to others. The shaman is the 'maker', and the Greek *poeitas*, the word for 'poet', means 'maker'. The shaman, like the artist, dreams society's dreams (we see van Gogh doing this very clearly). The shaman is the technician of ecstasy, to use Eliade's term. Robert Graves spoke of the 'poetic trance', that shamanic state in which the writer creates.

SPIRITUALITY AND INVISIBILITY

Any religious painting is an interface between the human the divine, between the secular and the sacred. It is an uneasy, ambiguous relationship. The painting is both a mundane object, a bit of wood, canvas and pigment, purchased in the dusty streets, brought back to the studio, and put together by the painter. The painting-as-object is thoroughly secular, thoroughly ordinary. Yet it is also a sacred object, a piece of magic. The painter works with solid, real materials to create something that is illusion, not very solid, really; the painting is something unreal, insubstantial, ethereal, impossible to grasp, something powerful though; in short, something *magical*.

Painters of all eras wrestle with these physical, semantic, psychological, æsthetic and metaphysical tensions. The tensions between abstraction and representation, between 'illusion' and 'reality', between colour and 'life'. The religious painter has to deal with the ever-impossible task: the depiction of the invisible and the unknown. On one level, John Ruskin's view of J.M.W. Turner's art as penetrating through to some mystical Beyond also applies to van Gogh. Van Gogh's art is regarded as penetrating Nature, to reveal something of the spiritual essence beyond:

whatever Turner's or Ruskin's reticences about the God of Christendom, Ruskin was on to something fundamental when he argued that what Turner reveals about nature does not stop at appearances but reaches through and beyond them to a spiritual vision of nature itself.[4]

This is a common view of art, that it can penetrate through the visible to the invisible. It is especially common around the time of Symbolism and early 20th century/ late 19th century art. The basic idea is that there is an 'essence of things', as the sculptor Constantin Brancusi put it, that the artist can grasp if s/he is good enough, and bring out in her/his art.

We find this idea in Paul Klee, Max Beckmann, Brancusi, Arthur Rimbaud, Charles Baudelaire and others. It is worth looking at the artists who parallel van Gogh's thinking on reaching the essence or spirit of things. Brancusi reduced organic, natural forms to 'essences'. Yet he maintained that his sculpture was not abstract. Kandinsky said that abstraction = realism,[5] and this is true of Brancusi, who vigorously stressed the realism of his works:

> They are imbeciles who call my work abstract; that which they call abstract is the most realist, because what is real is not the exterior form but the idea, the essence of things.[6]

It is a quest for things, for things-in-themselves, as Existential philosophers such as Sartre and Heidegger put it, the 'thingness' of Rainer Maria Rilke. It is van Gogh's quest: for the Real, the Superreal of mysticism. The 'things' of art are organic forms, not abstract ideas or abstruse conceptualizations. As Henry Moore wrote, and he could have been talking of van Gogh, a 'sculptor is a person obsessed with the form and shape of things...the shape of anything and everything.'[7] Van Gogh and Brancusi denied the urge towards abstraction: a new, visionary realism was van Gogh's goal, his Grail. The quest for the 'spirit of a place' that is van Gogh's quest is derived ultimately from Plato's ideal philosophy.

For Plato, there is some ultimate or absolute, something definite and solid at the bottom of things. Brancusi followed Plato's notion of Ideal Forms and essences, reducing his art further and further, so that he could get as close as possible to the 'essence of the thing'. It is a process of Neoplatonic purification, as Dorothy Adlow noted when she visited Brancusi's studio in 1925:

> Brancusi has purified his sculpture of every attracting feature. He has swept out of his plan every motive that might distract him or the observer from what he considers the central idea...He has tried to make of his sculpture a working philosophy. He calls it the philosophy of Plato.[8]

There is a parallel to this purification in poets and novelists. French writers, such as Stendhal, Flaubert, Gide and Beckett spoke of wanting to clear away all the garbage that gets in the way of purity of expression. Samuel Beckett, for instance, steadily pared away his language, moving from the relatively conventional novel forms of books such as *Mercier and Camier* through the reduced vocabulary and syntax of *The Trilogy* to the severely reduced poesie of *Company* and *Still*. For some artists, nothing must get in the way of expression of the idea or emotion.

Rainer Maria Rilke, who worked with Rodin, widely regarded as the 'father' of 20th century sculpture, wrote illuminatingly of surfaces and essences. Of the transformation of his art in his *Neue Gedichte*, which was a breakthrough, Rilke wrote that 'it had to arrive at the essence.'[9] And in a fragment of his greatest work, the *Duino Elegies*, Rilke writes of 'the infinite thereness of statues', a thought that many artists, from Michelangelo to Brancusi, or philosophers from Plotinus to Nietzsche would agree with (in ib., 215).

Rilke's notion of 'Kunst-Ding' or innerness or thingness, also called *innigkeit*, has much in common with Vincent van Gogh's notion of the underlying spirituality of the world. The poet's task, Rilke said, was to capture the 'thingness' of an object, without ornamentation or rhetoric, rather in the manner that Cézanne did with his still life paintings. Van Gogh's aim is also that of Rilke, who wrote:

> When I attempt to visualize my task, it becomes clear to me that it is not people about whom I have to speak, but things. Things. When I say the word (do you hear?) there is a silence; the silence which surrounds things. All movement subsides and becomes contour. And out of past and future time something permanent is formed: space, the great calm of objects which knows no urge.[10]

Rilke's spatial mysticism has is a poetic, lingual equivalent of post-Symbolist painting. For Rilke, expressing a sense of space meant the poem could expand the Within outwards, towards the "Open": Van Gogh too speaks of mystical openness, though he calls it 'infinity'. Some of van Gogh's painting explore a Rilkean 'openness'. In poems such as 'The Panther', 'Archaic Torso of Apollo' and 'Blue Hydrangea', Rilke, like van Gogh, tried to present things as they really were. This extract from 'The Bowl of Roses' demonstrates Rilke's poetic goals, and provides a poetic equivalent of van Gogh's still life paintings and flowerpieces:

> Living in silence, endless opening out,
> space being used, but without space being taken
> from that space which the things around diminish;
> absence of outline, like untinted groundwork
> and mere Within; so much so strangely tender
> and self-illumined – to the very verge: –
> where do we know anything like this?[11]

Rilke's quest for mystical innerness and van Gogh's goal of finding the spirit of a place have affinities with Heidegger's notion of Being and presence, with James Joyce's idea of the æsthetic 'epiphany' of authentic art, with Lawrence Durrell's poetic concept of the heraldic 'sigil' or signature of a thing, and with *samma-dassana* of Zen Buddhism. D.T. Suzuki writes:

Seeing is experiencing, seeing things in their states of suchness (*tathata*) or is-ness. Buddha's whole philosophy comes from this "seeing", this experiencing.[12]

Brancusi speaks of a similar mystical 'seeing', where the viewer of his sculptures see not simply beautiful surfaces, but essences. He writes:

What is real is not the external form, but the essence of things. Starting from this truth it is impossible for anyone to express anything luscious and real by imitating its exterior surface.[13]

Max Beckmann, a painter that has much in common with Vincent van Gogh (the sympathy for/ with Christ, the Expressonist gestures, the tragic, Nietzschean view of life, the use of vivid colour) aimed to get at the 'magic of reality', as he called it, and to make it visible in art:

What I want to show in my work is the idea which hides itself behind so-called reality. I am seeking for the bridge which leads from the visible to the invisible, like the famous cabalist who once said: "If you want to get hold of the invisible, you must penetrate as deeply as possible into the visible." My aim is always to get hold of the magic of reality and to transfer this reality into painting – to make the invisible.[14]

Any number of poets have felt the same thing – that there is an invisible presence or essence underneath the surface of life that is magical. Novalis, Goethe and Heinrich Heine among German poets, wrote of the invisible magic underneath life, while other poets, such as Dante, Shakespeare, Shelley, Rimbaud, Akhmatova and Scève have explored the invisible realm.

The poet can delve in a particular way, using the magic of words – a poet such as D.H. Lawrence can speak of the mystery of seeds, for instance, which illuminate much of the enigmas of birth, life and death. The painter has a daunting task in making the invisible visible. Like van Gogh, Beckmann was sensitive to the strains of 'occultism' that are found in so much of late 19th century art. Beckmann was familiar with many areas of occultism and philosophy that are founded upon the notions of a poetic underworld: Indian religion, Gnosticism, Qabalism and Neo-platonism. [15]

In his lecture on painting, Beckmann describes his art as a van Goghian journey when he embarks on a work. First he creates a sense of space in which the self can blossom. The 'self', for Beckmann, is an essence in things; self or essence 'was only one form and is immortal' (op.cit., 188). Creating the right sense of space, a *religious* sense of space, is crucial: 'Space, and space again, is the infinite deity which surrounds us and in which we are ourselves contained' says Beckmann, again echoing the philosophies of the Orient, in particular the spatial mysteries of the Hindu Brahma and the Chinese Tao. Painting is Beckmann's way of bringing together all these spiritual and spatial elements: 'when spiritual, metaphysical, material or immaterial events come into my life, I can only fix them by way of painting.' Gradually, through the process of painting, things begin to take shape spiritually and materially: 'Then shapes become beings and seem to comprehend me in the great void and uncertainty of the space which I call God.'

Beckmann's poetics of painting pivots around the relationship between the material and the mystical. Always he emphasizes the importance in painting of making tangible the spiritual dimension: 'Imagination is perhaps the most decisive characteristic of mankind. My dream is the imagination of space – to change the optical impression of the world of objects by a transcendental arithmetic progress of the inner being. That is the precept.'

Oscar Kokoschka, who, as with the other Expressionists, shares Vincent van Gogh's tragic sensitivity, wrote of the importance of the inner vision:

The state of awareness of visions is not one in which we are remembering or perceiving. It is rather a level of consciousness at which we experience visions within ourselves...The effect is such that the visions seem actually to modify one's consciousness, at least in respect of everything which their own form proposes as their pattern and significance. This change in oneself, which follows on the vision's penetration of one's very soul, produces the state of awareness, of expectancy. As the same time there is an outpouring of feeling into the image which becomes, as it were, the soul's plastic embodiment.[16]

This is also Vincent van Gogh's ethic: that art interrogates the invisible, tries to make visible the invisible. Or as Paul Klee, one of the masters of interiority, put it: 'Art does not reproduce the visible; rather, it makes visible.'[17]

A modern landscape artist, Richard Long, speaks in poetic, religious terms of his art which chime with van Gogh's views: 'art should be a religious experience' (in Wheeler, 264). Although his sculptures alter the world – no *object* can avoid altering the world – Long maintains that he takes his cue from the landscape, as van Gogh did, instead of imposing on it 'from outside', as it were: 'I use the world as I find it'.[18] Like van Gogh's ideas on art, Long's views have something in common with Zen, Taoism, shamanism and Western magic.[19] The sculpture and the place are one, in a mystical relationship, as Long points out in his writings:

The material and the idea are of the place; sculpture and place are one, the same. The place is as far as the eye can see from the sculpture. The place for a sculpture is found by walking. Some works are a succession of particular places along a walk, e.g. *Milestones*. In this work, the walking, the places and the stones all have equal importance.[20]

Both Vincent van Gogh and land artists such as Richard Long have the *participation mystique* with the Earth, with places and atmospheres and organic materials, that the archaic peoples of the world had (and have). Constantin Brancusi too spoke of this primal, 'primitive' relationship with the world, which renders his sculpture 'archaic', for some people (although the term 'archaic' is used sometimes in the anthropological sense, but more often in the pseudo-psychological sense beloved of art critics). It is a pre-institutionalized, pre-pagan and pantheistic rapport with the world, deliberately eschewing dogma, doctrine and manifestos.

Vincent van Gogh moves out of his time, outside of French art, or the Parisian or modernist avant garde, outside of European art, in his quest for the 'essence of things'. There is always a striving for some realm greater than his immediate *milieu* of the last half of the 19th century. Van Gogh's art is simultaneously of his era (following on from Delacroix, Millet, Courbet, Corot, Manet, Monet, French naturalism and Impressionism), and archaic, shamanic, magical, Platonic, mystical. Though van Gogh's art is mainly figurative and representational, it points towards 20th century abstraction, towards an otherness that is utterly *real*, an abstraction that is pure reality. Nature not artifice, reality not fantasy.

PROVENCE

A character in the novel *Livia*, by Lawrence Durrell, muses thus:

> Closing his eyes he seemed to see in memory all the black magnetism of the dark light which shone out of the [Provençal] earth, whether among these trees and vines or out of the bald garrigues and pebbled hills with their crumbling shale valleys. Among these rambling dormitories of shards Van Gogh had hunted the demon of his black noonday sun – and found it in madness. Only when one was here did one realise how truthful to the place was his account of it.[21]

Durrell loved South France, and spent the second half of his life living in Provence. As well as setting some of his fiction in Provence, he also wrote a book about the region. Speaking of the South of France, van Gogh wrote:

Vincent van Gogh

Nature here is so *extraordinarily* beautiful! Everywhere and over all the vault the sky is a marvellous blue, and the sun sheds a radiance of pale sulphur. (no. 490)

For Vincent van Gogh, Provence was 'the land of rose laurels and a sun like sulphur' (Lassaigne, 76). He spoke of the 'rich colour and rich sun of the glorious South' (no. 477).

IV

WORKS

There is something melancholy, even depressing, about Vincent van Gogh's early works. It is a combination of his treatment of the subjects, the choice of subjects, and the subjects themselves. The early drawings are marked by a heavy, shadowy, Rembrandtian treatment. The drawings of a corner of a garden, the Jewish quarter of The Hague, a road in Loosduinen (1881-2) are all dim, dour images. These are not van Gogh's most sorrowful pictures, though. The drawings and paintings of people in various states of abjection, poverty, boredom and pain are the most saddening sights in van Gogh's *œuvre*. He drew pictures of old men with their heads in their hands, leaning forward on chairs; he drew peasants digging and gardening; he drew miner's wives carrying sacks; he drew a peasant woman binding wheat; he drew a man cutting wood; he drew a group of people eating potatoes; he drew a woman winding bobbins; he drew an old man reeling yarn. All these pictures of people toiling away are portrayed with a tender realism that is both heartening and disheartening. The tenderness of the artist is heartwarming, but the working conditions of those 'peasants' is so sordid and horrible. This is the heart-wrenching project of van Gogh's early drawings and paintings, this unadorned look at the working conditions of the poor and the peasant class. Van Gogh's depictions of poor folk are as powerful as Hogarth's or those of anonymous 19th century engravers and woodcut artists. Heads down, expressionless, backs bent, in their white bonnets or caps, van Gogh's workers keep at their labour with a grim determination, in dirty, squalid interiors. These interiors contain ancient chairs and tables, but little else. There are gloomy still lifes of pots, jars, pipe cases, beer mugs, sacks, clogs and bottles.

The influence of the Dutch and Flemish Old Masters, as well as Rembrandt, is very much in evidence in van Gogh's early works. One wonders what state the van Gogh legend would be in if van Gogh had stopped painting with *The Potato Eaters*. There is nothing amateurish or unaccomplished about these works (*The Potato Eaters, Head of a Peasant Woman* (O), *The Antwerp Quay, Peasant Woman Sweeping* (O), *Still Life with Open Bible, The Loom* (O), *Peasant Woman By the Fireplace* (Musée d'Orsay)), but the vision and radiance of the later works (*Wheatfield with Cypress Tree, The Postman Joseph Roulin, Outdoor Café by Night*) far transcends the dark, gloomy introspection of the early works.

By the mid-1880s van Gogh's palette was lightening, but many of the works were still shot through with an introspective melancholy (in, for example, the wistful landscapes of *Autumn Landscape* (Cambridge), *Autumn Landscape with Four Trees* (O), *Autumn Landscape at Dusk* (Utrecht) and *Lane with Poplars* (Rotterdam)). Examples of van Gogh's lighter colouration of the mid-1880s include the studies he made of plaster statues (*Plaster Statuette of a Female Torso, Plaster Statuette of a Kneeling Man, Plaster Statuette of a Male Torso* and *Plaster Statuette of a Horse* – each version is in Amsterdam).

Vincent van Gogh, though he seemed to be 'isolated' in Provence from the centres of culture (such as Paris), kept up with current debates in the arts, as well as discussing much with painters such as Gauguin. He spoke respectfully about his contemporaries, such as Manet, Seurat and Gauguin. The heritage of painting was deeply important to him too – he thought so much of earlier painters, he incorporated their motifs into his work, or even based his own paintings on theirs – he painted works 'after' Millet, Rembrandt and Delacroix, among others.

> When I realize the worth and originality and the superiority of Delacroix and Millet, for instance, then I am bold enough to say – yes, I am something, I can do something. But must have a foundation in those artists, and then produce the little I am capable of in the same direction. (no. 605)

The sheer number of paintings after Millet is a testament to van Gogh's admiration of the painter: there are the various *Sowers (After Millet)*, plus *Evening: The Watch (After Millet)*, *The Woodcutter (After Millet)*, *Noon: Rest From Work (After Millet)*, *First Steps (After Millet)*, *The Plough and the Harrow (After Millet)*, *Morning: Peasant Couple Going to Work (After Millet)*, *The Shepherdess (After Millet)*, *Evening: The End of the Day (After Millet)*, *The Sheep-Shearers (After Millet)*, *Peasant Woman Cutting Straw (After Millet)* and *The Thresher (After Millet)*.

The accounts of his visits to museums and galleries in his letters attest to his love of contemporary painting, and the Old Masters. Of a visit to the museums of Antwerp, van Gogh spoke highly of painters such as Rembrandt ('*very* beautiful'), Hals, de Vos, Ruisdael, Massys and van Eyck (no. 436).

Vincent van Gogh's sketchbooks attest to his determined study of form and art history. There are a surprising number of life studies, of torsos, breasts, arms, legs, though van Gogh is not associated primarily with nudes or the human figure. There are also sketches that van Gogh made in museums such as the Louvre. There are many studies made in the open air, of people standing and sitting in parks (such as the Luxembourg Gardens and the Tuileries in Paris). Many of van Gogh's sketches were used directly as the basis for paintings. The sketch for *The Town Hall of Auvers-sur-Oise*, for instance (F 1630 *recto*) does not differ that much from the painting, though the painting (private collection) does contain elements of the Bastille Day celebrations (flags, Chinese lanterns).

TREES

One of my favourite paintings is one of Vincent van Gogh's most 'Oriental', or Japanese: this is the *Branches of an Almond Tree in Bloom* (painted around 20 February 1890, one of the last from Saint-Rémy). Against a clear blue sky, the pure blue and turquoise sky of Provence, van Gogh depicts the upper branches of the almond trees. Van Gogh manages to convey the wonder of blossom, which only lasts a week or two each year. As an 'outdoor' artist, someone who haunted outdoor spaces for hours on end, van Gogh would have been well aware of the changing seasons. One of the most dramatic manifestations of Nature's seasonal cycle is the appearance of blossom in Spring. It was inevitable that van Gogh should paint the wonder of a tree in blossom, that silent (but very 'loud', in terms of colour of light) occurrence. What van Gogh does is to cut out extraneous details – other trees, hills, grass, fences, buildings, animals – and concentrates just on the branches and the blossom and the sky. Such a concentration of energy on a small portion of the world results in a painting which contains a lot of energy and light. Van Gogh says he created *Almond Tree in Blossom* 'in utter peace and quiet, with the greatest certainty of brush strokes'. The exuberance of the painting may stem partly from it being intended as a gift for the birth of van Gogh's brother's baby. The white almond blossom is dotted around the painting and, like confetti, gives a celebratory air to the picture. *Branches of an Almond Tree in Blossom* is also one of van Gogh's flattest paintings, with very little suggestion of the illusion of depth, apart from the fact that one branch is seen behind the ones in front. The abstraction of the painting looks forward not only to the Fauvists and Cubists, but beyond them to the Abstract Expressionists.

Another tree in blossom was painted in March 1888 in Arles (*Peach Tree in Blossom*, O). The tone is very pale, with scarcely a tone darker than the mid-pink used for the blossoms. The first impressions of the cloudy and blue sky, the whitey-pink of the blossom and the near-white of the ground is quickly altered when one considers just how many colours van Gogh used in this painting. There is red, yellow, green, grey, dark blue, turquoise, leaf green, light orange, sepia, scarlet and white – and that's just for the ground area underneath the tree. *Peach Tree in Blossom* is one of van Gogh's least troubled works. It speaks of calm and optimism. The tree in *The Mulberry Tree* (Norton Simon Museum of Art, Pasadena) painted in October 1889 at Saint-Rémy, explodes outwards in every direction. Each branch is constructed from van Gogh curving lines, the fiery appearance of the tree is exaggerated by the colours: yellow, orange and red for the tree, again a mid-blue sky. Although the landscape is complex – interlocking fields, hills and hedges – *The Mulberry Tree* has a remarkable directness, because van Gogh has placed the tree dead centre again. Such a simple design might not work if it wasn't carried off with van Gogh's brilliant colouration and energetic lines.

La Crau with Peach Trees in Blossom has the blossom painted on last, as so often in Vincent van Gogh's art, with large dabs of white paint. The sky is also constructed from short horizontal brushstrokes, in the Georges Seurat manner. *View of Arles, Orchard in Bloom with Poplars in the Foreground* (Munich) is a painting teeming with life: the poplars in the foreground have new shoots and branches growing out of their trunks; in the orchard, the trees are blooming with white blossom, while below is lush grass.

View of Arles, Orchard in Bloom with Poplars in the Foreground seems to be a painting in which the upward thrust of Nature, the primal urge to grow, is deeply felt. The sense of the sap rising is enhanced by the brushstrokes, most of which are vertical. The foliage in the painting seems to be leaping skyward. Other notable studies of trees in blossom include *Orchard in Blossom* (New York), *Orchard with Blossoming Apricot Trees* (A), *Apricot Trees in Blossom* (Switzerland), against a brooding sky, *Orchard with Peach Tree in Blossom* (New York), *Orchard in Blossom, Bordered by Cypresses* (O), with a spectral, egg-shell blue sky, and *Orchard in Blossom* (Edinburgh). Two blossom paintings in the Rijksmuseum Vincent van Gogh in Amsterdam view the tree from underneath, the canvas tilted upwards to catch the branches against the pale blue sky.

Van Gogh's paintings of Les Alyscamps contain figures in a park setting, but the trees are van Gogh's main subject; in the Lausanne *Les Alyscamps* the path is shown moving off at a low diagonal, but in the other *Les Alyscamps* (private collection) van Gogh set his easel up in the centre of the path, producing a stately air: the presence of the grey sky and the sarcophagi give the picture a solemn look, which's disrupted by the exuberance with which van Gogh paints the soaring verticality of the poplars. In *Lilacs*, painted in May 1889 at Saint-Rémy, various bushes, trees and flowers overflow through the whole painting, so there is only room for a small portion of the Provençal sky.

The trees that van Gogh painted in the garden of the Saint-Paul Hospital (Los Angeles and private collection) are backed by a radiant sky and ochre soil. In these paintings, entitled *Trees in the Garden of Saint-Paul Hospital*, van Gogh places saturated colours – deep greens, blues, yellow and brown – which're set next to each other. In a couple of later *Gardens of Saint-Paul Hospital* (Essen and A), van Gogh positions his easel so that it faces away from the building, towards the distant hills and sky. A watery, wintry sky of lilac, grey and lemon yellow forms the background to another study of trees.

Some of the most 'abstract' of Vincent van Gogh's paintings are his studies of ivy and undergrowth. For the scenic painter looking for 'pretty' views, there seems to be nothing attractive about these shadowy spaces underneath the trees (in *Undergrowth with Ivy* and *Tree Trunks with Ivy*, both Amsterdam, and *Tree Trunks with Ivy* (O)). Yet, whether van Gogh paints them in sunshine or on an overcast day, he finds much there to occupy him. The most 'abstract' of the ivy and undergrowth pictures is *Undergrowth with Ivy*, in which green is practically the only colour employed, with white and black as secondary hues.

The drawings of trees in blossom are as substantial as the paintings. One of Vincent van Gogh's special gifts was to be able to isolate his subject from its surroundings without displacing it, so it would not look out of place. His trees (or fields, or flowers, or whatever) have a certain amount of space around them, in order to encourage the viewer to consider the subject. Van Gogh sets up his viewpoint (or easel) some thirty or so feet from the tree, so that a detailed scrutiny of the tree can be made, but a sense of objectivity and distance is also retained.

Van Gogh treats trees as figures: he paints and draws the trees in their fields as if he is approaching the human figure. His trees take up the whole frame, from top to bottom, extending outwards to the sides of the frame. Few artists have portrayed trees as lyrically and sympathetically as van Gogh. One thinks of Corot, with his dark green, soft, wind-blown trees in out-of-the-way meadows. In Corot and van Gogh, the *space around and under* a tree is poetically treated, as well as the tree itself. The space under and around a tree is important, and in van Gogh and Corot, the sense of the shade and the umbrella covering of the branches is lovingly described. It's an important point, to portray the space under and around a tree: before this time, painters had so often treated trees as decoration, or as two dimensional shapes. In van Gogh, and in Corot, trees become rooted in the earth, and one can explore the spaces underneath the trees.

OLIVE GROVES

At Saint-Rémy, Vincent van Gogh produced a series of fifteen canvases of olive groves. These are made powerful by their simplicity: van Gogh has rationalized the landscape of the trees, forming three groups of colours and objects. The straw-coloured ground and grass; the dark green of the olive leaves; and the eternal azure of the Provençal sky. In the first of the *Olive Orchards* (June 1889, O) every brushstroke is curving and thick with paint. Van Gogh works wet in wet, and quickly, piling on the marks with self-assurance and verve. The half-moon shaped brushmarks cover the whole canvas, so the earth, grass, trees and sky are all unified by the dynamism of van Gogh's physical handling of the paint. The leaves of the olive trees curl up and disappear into the curves of the sky. The grass, yellow and white in the sunlight, viridian and leaf green in the shade, merges with the tree trunks and the lower levels of the olive leaves. The result is that *Olive Grove* is an amazingly energetic painting, all twists and turns, the energy of the gnarled and twisted olive trees is enhanced by the kinetic brushwork. Although the scene may be the epitome of tranquillity – an olive grove snoozing in the midday heat – in van Gogh's hands it becomes a mass of writhing vigour.

Another olive grove painting (*Women Picking Olives*, a.k.a. *The Olive Orchard*, Washington), makes the film of dusty and grey light that van Gogh saw as an essential ingredient of the olive groves even more pronounced (a similar light is found in *Olive Grove*, A, while other versions of *The Olive Pickers* include the ones in New York, in Otterlo, and in the collection of Walter H. Annenberg). The olive trees' leaves are given a light green colour with a lot of grey in between them, to indicate their silvery undersides. As with other olive grove pictures, the little curved brushstrokes in the sky continue on the landscape, and in the olive leaves. This achieves that characteristic molten or mobile van Gogh effect, where every object is endowed with energy and liveliness. Van Gogh depicts the world with a mass of short, curved or straight brushstrokes, so every area of the painting seems busy and kinetic. Sometimes, this effect can appear overwhelming, in some of the *Road with Cypress* paintings, or in the *Wheatfields* series.

In the Washington *Women Picking Olives*, the use of short brushstrokes fills the picture with energy which seems at odd with the subject matter. For the colour and light of *The Olive Orchard* is very subdued; it is an overcast, dull day, shadowless, with none of the golden light or intense colouration that characterizes van Gogh's other Provençal paintings. Even on the dullest of days, though, van Gogh seems to be saying in *Women Picking Olives*, Nature is teeming with energy. In fact, the only objects in *The Olive Orchard not* painted with van Gogh's short brushstrokes, are the three women. The Kansas *Olive Grove* is a much warmer rendering, the key colour being green modulated by yellow. On the left are poppies.

In the Minneapolis *Olive Trees with Yellow Sky and Sun* Vincent van Gogh combines the olive grove image with one of his favourite motifs – the sun, seen face-on, in the centre of the painting. The sky in *Olive Trees with Yellow Sky and Sun* is nothing but gold, recalling J.M.W. Turner in what Thomas Hardy called his 'late, mad' phase. In *Olive Grove: Orange Sky* (Göteborgs Konstmuseum) van Gogh again depicts the olive trees at sunset, with a sky moving from red (top right) through green and blue to yellow and orange (centre left). The colouration of *Olive Trees: Bright Blue Sky* (Edinburgh) is quite different from other *Olive Grove* paintings: the soil alone is composed of purple, ochre, yellow, white, red, grey, black, khaki and brown.

CYPRESS TREES

One of van Gogh's most typical motifs, one that is instantly recognisable, is his cypress trees. Typically, they are dark, dominant shapes, often taking up the whole height of his horizontal format canvases, often placed to one side, left or right. In his letters, van Gogh compares the line and proportion of the cypress tree to an Egyptian obelisk. He goes on to write:

> And the green has a quality of such distinction.
> It is a splash of *black* in a sunny landscape, but it is one of the most interesting black notes, and the most difficult to hit off exactly that I can imagine.
> But then you must see them against the blue, *in* the blue rather. (25 June 1889, no. 596)

Van Gogh's cypress trees are a mass of writhing lines and dark tones. They are so much like black flames, curling upwards from the earth. Easy to see how the fiery patterns of van Gogh's cypresses recall D.H. Lawrence's descriptions of flame-like trees. Vincent van Gogh's trees are domineering, elemental forms, very often the darkest tones in his paintings (as in *The Starry Night*). In *Cypresses* (Metropolitan Museum, New York), painted in Saint-Rémy in June 1889, the tree are central an huge. Every brushstroke is curved: there are no straight lines here: the field is a mass of curving grass, the hills undulate like snakes, the sky is vigorously described with circular impasto, and the dark viridian green trees are thick with half-circles of oil. In *Cypresses with Two Female Figures* the row of trees is again central, with the surrounding grass and bushes more defined. Despite the presence of the women and houses beyond, the real subject of the painting, as with Corot's pastoral scenes, is the landscape.

The drawings of the cypresses are as impressive as the paintings. The black chalk and pen and ink drawing of two women in a field (O) shows a line of some four or so cypresses, each one a column of rippling, fiery forms. One of the most powerful of van Gogh's images of cypress trees is also one of his most apocalyptic paintings, *Road with Man Walking, Carriage, Cypress, Star and Crescent Moon* (O) the last painting van Gogh made at Saint-Rémy, some two months before his death. The cypress towers over everything in the painting, from the golden wheatfield on the left, to the strange, snake-like perspective of the near-empty country road. The pattern of the brushstrokes in *Road with Man Walking, Carriage, Cypress, Star and Crescent Moon* is very pronounced, as in the late *Wheatfield with Crows*. The leaves of the tree leap outwards from the trunk into the sky, while the white road seems to be turning into a flood of white dust. The sky in *Road with Man Walking, Carriage, Cypress, Star and Crescent Moon* is one van Gogh's most animated, with yellow, white, turquoise, green, violet and cream mixed in vigorously. Curiously, the crescent moon is seen to the *left* of the sun, which is not usual at sunset. Also, the crescent is seen shining on its right, away from the sun. These odd features of the opposed sun and moon recall the penchant in Renaissance *Crucifixion* paintings to deliberately reverse the sun and moon on either side of the Cross, in order to emphasize the apocalyptic nature of the Crucifixion scene. Van Gogh's *Road with Man Walking, Carriage, Cypress, Star and Crescent Moon* seems to unconsciously evoke this Renaissance symbolism, with the dark, brooding green-black cypress tree admirably standing in for the Cross and Saviour. These crescent moon paintings do appear to be simultaneously 'realist' and visionary, naturalistic and expressionistic; it's hard not to see paintings such as *Landscape with Couple Walking and Crescent Moon* (1890, Museu de Arte de São Paulo) without associating it with symbolism.

WHEATFIELDS

No painter, before or since Vincent van Gogh, has made depictions of wheatfields and cornfields so much their own. Van Gogh's paintings of wheatfields are some of his most radiant images. They allow some of his favourite colours, yellow and gold, to run riot. In the *Wheatfields*, van Gogh does indeed run riot, layering on the yellow and white and orange. He must have used umpteen tubes of yellow and white. Many of van Gogh's paintings are soaked in yellow – such as *Vincent's House in Arles*; *Sunset: Wheat Fields near Arles* (Winterhur); *Arles: View From the Wheatfields* (Musée Rodin, Paris); *Les Alyscamps* (Lausanne); the floor of *The Night Café* (New Haven); the sky in *Street in Saintes-Maries* (private collection); the chair in *Vincent's Chair with His Pipe* (London); the lemon yellow sky in *A Meadow in the Mountains: Les Mas de Saint-Paul* (O); the backgrounds of many of the still lifes; and the sky in *The Raising of Lazarus (After Rembrandt)*. It is one of the most distinctive of van Gogh's colours, so one can speak of a 'van Gogh yellow', just as one can speak of a Matisse red (in *The Red Studio*) or a Rothko maroon (in the Houston and Seagram murals) or a Whistler deep blue (in the *Nocturnes*). Yellow, too, is dominant in many of the portraits; the bright yellow backgrounds in *L'Arlésienne* (New York), *Mother*

Roulin with Her Baby (Philadelphia), *Portrait of Madame Augustine Roulin* (Winterhur), *Portrait of the Postman Joseph Roulin* (Winterhur); the yellow jacket in the *portrait of Arman Roulin* (Essen); the yellow hat in the *Portrait of Patience Escalier* (Pasadena), and in many of the self-portraits. One can perceive very rapidly a van Gogh painting in amongst other paintings on a gallery wall, because of this distinctive use of yellowy-gold. This colour is just as much a part of van Gogh's style as his swirling brushstrokes, or heavy impasto.

> I am working on two landscapes... views taken in the hills, one is the country that I see from the window of my bedroom. In the foreground, a field of wheat ruined and hurled to the ground by a storm. A boundary wall and beyond the grey foliage of a few olive trees, some huts and the hills. Then at the top of the canvas a great white and grey cloud floating in the azure. It is a landscape of extreme simplicity in colouring too... (no. 594)

Some of the wheatfield pictures have a very low viewpoint (perhaps made with the painter sitting on the grass) so that the ears and stalks of wheat tower above the eyeline (as in *Green Ears of Wheat*, 1888, Israel Museum, Jerusalem). In *Wheatfield with a Lark* (1887, A), the view is side-on to the edge of the field, the picture divided into three horizontal bands: blue sky, green wheat and yellowed grass.

One of the more majestic wheatfield pictures is *Wheatfield with Reaper* (Folkwang Museum, Essen) a landscape-format painting, in van Gogh's usual composition (landscape taking up two thirds of the frame). The Otterlo *Wheatfield* is a similar composition of yellow and gold. Forget that the reaper symbolized death for van Gogh, and luxuriate in the acres of golden wheat, which's being harvested. Van Gogh spends much of his time in the manufacture of this painting with making short brushstrokes in yellow and orange. These strokes do not depict each individual stem of wheat – they would be far too thin for van Gogh's purpose – but the impression of them. The field, as portrayed by the artist, is one vast mass of golden plants. This is partly why we speak of van Gogh as a 'visionary' painter. His aim is not simply to conjure up the wheatfield as a 'reality', nor to give an 'impression' of it, as the Impressionists might have done, but to express the effect of the wheatfield on him. Van Gogh's *Wheatfields* are portrayals of a subjective experience, which later became known as 'Express-ionist'. The painting hovers between 'realism' and 'expressionism', between 'reality' and 'abstraction'. The terms have to be put into quotations marks because they are so elusive, ambiguous, confused terms. Van Gogh's works are simultaneously 'realist' and 'abstract', as all art is.

Van Gogh's talent was to show what it was he was interested in so poignantly, what aspect of the world, what colours, shapes, sights and sounds. It is one thing to point out the wheatfield, or to see it, but quite another thing to paint it, and to paint it well. Van Gogh does not simply set up his easel and knock off a painting of a wheatfield, in the manner of a Sunday afternoon amateur artist. In the *Wheatfields* and other paintings, we can see van Gogh questing for something, trying to bring something into life on the canvas. The paintings are the result of his response to the landscape, an experience which can easily be interpreted as visionary' or 'religious'. For at the centre of *Wheatfield with Reaper* is an enormous yellow sun. Again, in previous painters, this sun would be discreetly small, and probably not even in the frame at all. Not only does van Gogh paint the sun, he makes it massive. Again, there is the sense of compressed space, such as one sees in long photographic telephoto or zoom lenses. All the elements of the landscape are brought right up onto the front picture plane. Spatial depth is weak, with the hills in violet and grey. The field, from front to back, is rendered as a vertical froth of yellow and gold. The reaper works amongst the sheaves of wheat as if he's treading in a golden cloud, or floating on an angry yellow sea. The painting is full of energy, like most of van Gogh's paintings, with vigorous brush strokes moving diagonally across the sky.

Evening Landscape with Rising Moon (O) offers an equally visionary scene: with the Provençal sun gone down, the moon rises in the stillness of the twilight. Van Gogh's masterful painting captures the quiet magic of the time between day and night, in summer, with the haystacks standing silently in the empty field. What is striking about *Evening Landscape with Rising Moon* is the sheer size of the moon, as well as its bright orange hue. The moon looms over the hill, looking more like the sun than the sun itself.

The series of paintings of wheatfields, made in the environs of Saint-Rémy, are some of Vincent van Gogh's most characteristic as well as lyrical works. A sense of space and light infuses these paintings. Van Gogh's painterly technique responds to the landscape with a suppleness and ease. The black chalk and pen drawings of the wheatfields reveal the same skill, control and relaxation. The drawings allow the viewer to examine the full range of marks van Gogh makes in a composition: dots for flowers; vigorous curved verticals for grasses; thick black serpent-like marks for the cypress; crests and stipples for the hills, just like waves on the sea; fine curves for the clouds. In the oils, these marks are exaggerated, so that the energy they contain is heightened, sometimes to a degree of extreme vitality.

The Zurich *Wheatfields with Cypresses*, like the London painting, anchors the composition with a wide expanse of yellow wheat, with the ubiquitous cypress on one side. Every brushstroke emphasizes the movement of the air: the sky is especially flame-rich, with turquoise and cerulean swirls interspersing billows of white for the clouds. In the Boston *Field with Ploughman and Mill*, the field is split into strips of gold and dark soil. In *Mountain Landscape Behind Saint-Paul Hospital* (in Copenhagen) van Gogh paints a vast white cumulus cloud sweeping over the low hills.

A *Wheatfield with Cypresses* painting in Prague (June 1889,

Národni Gallery) recreates beautifully the atmosphere of an overcast day in the countryside. The expanse of van Gogh wheatfield is muted: soft lemon and white and pale green does for the blooming field. Just off-centre, the cypress tree; the field is ringed with hedges and bushes. The sky here sets the tone for the painting: it is very light, and constructed from long horizontal brushstrokes, instead of van Gogh's more typical fretful short curves. The spears of the long-stemmed grass in the foreground do not alter the subdued mood of the painting either. *Green Wheatfields* (Paul Mellon collection) also depicts an overcast day – the sky awash with curling blue and white clouds.

A number of paintings of wheatfields follow the pattern of the London *Wheatfield with Cypresses*, with its pale blue cloudy sky and golden field. Some of the *Wheatfields* are intensely golden, such as *Wheat Stacks with Reaper* (Toledo Museum of Art), *Haystacks in Provence* (O)). *Sunset: Wheat Fields near Arles* (Winterhur), *Wheatfield with Sheaves* (Honolulu Academy of Arts) and the Israel Museum (Jerusalem) *Harvest in Provence* and *Wheatfield with the Alpilles Foothills in the Background*, which contrasts a swathe of bright green grass with the golden wheat. Not all the wheatfield pictures are golden and radiant: the Indianapolis Museum of Art *Enclosed Wheatfield with Peasant* (1889) depicts an overcast day with no overriding colour, as in the other *Wheatfields*. In *Wheatfield Behind Saint-Paul Hospital* (Virginia), the overcast light is lifted by the vast white cloud drifting over the hills.

A drawing of the wheatfield seen from Vincent van Gogh's window at the Saint-Rémy Hospital of Saint-Paul (1889) depicts a huge black cloud sailing towards and partially obliterating the bright sun. The drawing reminds the viewer that van Gogh must have seen many different weather changes from the window in Saint-Rémy. His art attests to many hours spent gazing at Nature and the weather. 'I devour nature ceaselessly.' (no. 531) Like other outdoor artists (from early Western landscape painters such as the Early Netherlandish Joachim Patinir or Albrecht Altdorfer to the British Romantics and the French Impressionists), van Gogh's landscapes are the outcome of many hours observing the changing seasons, skies and natural forms.

Noon Rest (1890, Musée d'Orsay) is one of Vincent van Gogh's many versions of Old Master paintings. One colour predominates: 'van Gogh yellow', here with brown, orange, white and grey added, to soften the brilliance of the yellow. The pulling back of the yellow and gold enhances the atmosphere of dusty corn. To contrast the profusion of gold, which takes up over three quarters of the painting, van Gogh employs a pale blue, for the sky, which is picked up in the clothes of the two snoozing farm workers. The air of midday rest after a morning's hard work is emphasized by the tools of the trade – scythes – which appear in the foreground, and the shoes, which have been kicked off by the man prior to stretching back onto the corn stack. Van Gogh rationalizes and simplifies Millet's painting, building up the elements he regards as important: the overall light of the painting, the key colours of yellow and blue, and the figures with their simple peasant clothes and accoutrements.

Two more yellow-soaked paintings after Millet of Vincent van Gogh's are the *Sower with Setting Sun*, made in Arles in 1888 (O and E.G. Bührle, Zurich). In both paintings, the figure is of secondary importance: what dominates the painting is an enormous golden sun, touching the horizon. Turner painted suns, so many of his paintings were made by staring into the sun, but he did not paint a sun quite like this.

In the Otterlo *Sower with Setting Sun (After Millet)*, van Gogh draws his brush many times through the wet yellow paint, so the lines and dabs of paint look like lines of light emanating from the nearby star. There is something simultaneously child-like and sophisticated about van Gogh's sun, about his pictures as a whole. He has painted the sun just as children of five and six draw suns at infant school, with spikes of light exploding in all directions. Van Gogh makes the whole sky turn yellow: not a part of it is any other colour. There is no carefully reproduced 'aerial effect', the blue-on-blue one is used to seeing in Renaissance paintings. There is no soft transformation from the golden aura of the sun to the pale blue above the horizon that one sees in the skies of Claude Lorrain or Nicholas Poussin. Van Gogh simply fills the entire sky with mid-yellow. The foreground of *Sower with Setting Sun* he fills with violet shadows, following traditional colour theory, but the way van Gogh dabs the violet straight on top of the orangey-brown colour of the field renders the violet shadows *in front of*, not behind or to one side, the objects they are meant to be shadowing. Again, van Gogh's visual perception produces dazzling art.

In the later *Sower with Setting Sun (After Millet)*, the view is as through a telephoto lens, with the sun a gigantic golden orb right behind the sower's head. Another *Sower (After Millet)*, in a private collection, is tonally light, with the field done in greys and violets, with a sky of pale lemon. The sower takes up most of the composition, his outstretched arm and determined walk are the subject of the picture.

When you are far enough away from a city or town to be able to see the sun go down behind a hill and not a skyscraper, tower block or building, it is a really impressive sight. You can't help staring at it as it edges towards the horizon, a molten constantly-burning fireball. The sun on the horizon at sunset is pure light. Our energy source. Our *source*, period. The origin of life on Earth, *et cetera*. People drive to hillside car parks just to see the sun setting; or they park atop cliffs, and stare glumly out to sea at eight on a Spring evening. No wonder, then, that such a magical sight should entrance van Gogh, and many a painter before and after him. Few painters, though, have caught the full trans-plendency of the sun like van Gogh. One thinks again of J.M.W. Turner, but few others.

The poet Rainer Maria Rilke wrote of Vincent van Gogh's

Vincent van Gogh

Landscape with Setting Sun:

> one of those landscapes he was always postponing and yet
> already painting again and again: a setting sun, a yellow, round
> fragment: against it, full of revolt, Blue, Blue, Blue, the slope of
> curved hills, divorced from the twilight by a strip of soothing
> pulsations (a river?), in which, transparent in darkly aged gold,
> in the slanted front third of the picture, you can make out a
> field and leaning groups of upright sheafs of corn. (1988, 62)

FLOWERS

One of Vincent van Gogh's most popular images is his *Irises* (May
1889, J. Paul Getty Museum, Malibu). It is an image that finds its
way into art posters, into art diaries and other merchandize. Van
Gogh's *Irises* are part of the populist mythology of his art. There
seems to be nothing 'threatening' or 'disturbing' about the flowers
and the painting. The *Irises* is a painting of van Gogh's late, mad
period, when he was at Saint-Rémy de Provence, yet it does not
speak of madness or the asylum. Rather, *Irises* speaks of a life-
affirming view of Nature, with the troubling aspects of life put
aside for the moment.

Critics get wet and drip lustfully over paintings such as the
Irises. Ingo Walther writes: '[t]he painting is crammed with the
ripe, moist excesses of nature' (65). One reading of van Gogh's (or
any painter's) flowerpieces is that they are sensual depictions of
already sensual objects (flowers). On their own, seen from a
certain (masculinist) perspective, flowers connote Nature in
abundance, a pastoral sublime, and of course a host of female/
feminine connotations (flower as womb, petals as labia, *et cetera*).
This view sees van Gogh's flowers as pure sex. That is, a sensual
depiction of an already sensual object. The art critic's description

of van Gogh's *Irises* as 'ripe, moist excesses' is pure sex, pure womb, art criticism seeing art as a labial caress. But *The Irises is* one of van Gogh's most accomplished depictions of nature, of Nature in abundance (not 'excess' – there is nothing 'excessive' about this natural group of blue irises. There is no 'excess' in Nature here (or anywhere), but a natural growth and flowering).

Van Gogh's *Irises* is lush in terms of colour and treatment. With his usual flair for composition, van Gogh fills the frame with sections of colour, each one complementing the others. Blue predominates. It presides over the central band of the painting, as well as the immediate foreground on the right. Next is the middle green of the flowers' leaves and stems. Iris blades are particularly beautiful, and van Gogh fondly describes each one. So the blue and green of the irises doesn't overwhelm the composition, the painter places bright red soil underneath them, and red flowers seen behind the irises. Then, to counterpoint these rich greens, blues and reds, van Gogh places a white iris on the left. The white petals counteract the forest of blue and green which takes up the right half of the painting. In *The Irises*, van Gogh demonstrates what a subtle sense of composition and proportion he has. If the general view of him is as a colourist, or a painter for whom colour was a religion, paintings such as *The Irises* or *Café Terrace at Night* or *Park With a Couple and a Blue Fir Tree* show how dexterously van Gogh handled composition. He has an intuitive feel for proportion and framing, knowing when to enlarge or diminish an area of colour or a shape, when to hold back with his colour, or when to saturate it. In the *Chestnut Trees in Blossom* paintings (South America and O), the trees are vast, taking up two-thirds of the composition, dwarfing the figures underneath. *The Irises* is one of those paintings which are saturated with colours, like *His Bedroom in Arles* and *Wheatfield with Crows*. In the Ottawa *Iris* (1889) the painter limits himself to one iris – the others have died or are in bud. The solitary blue flower is surrounded by lush green vegetation – the leaves and grasses are much more the subject of the painting than the iris.

Another study of irises (*Vase with Irises*, A and New York) takes the same format at the famous *Sunflower* series. The subject of the painting is the sheer abundance of Nature, with the soft blue of the irises pouring out of the vase, onto the sides of the vase and the table. The colours in the *Sunflowers* series are justifiably famous. It is this deep orange and yellow, perhaps *the* van Gogh colour, which makes the first impact with the *Sunflower* paintings. Van Gogh said that sunflowers were 'his' flower. In the London *Sunflowers*, van Gogh enhances the radiance of the orangey-yellow flowers by having not only the background in a muddier yellow, but also the table top (this also occurs in the versions of *Still Life: Vase with Fourteen Sunflowers* in Tokyo and A).

In the *Vase with Twelve Sunflowers* (Munich) the background is changed to a light sky blue, with the table a deeper hue of yellow. This is more in keeping with van Gogh's preference for employing the system of complementary colours, so that the pale blue provides a suitably 'passive' ground for the melodious passages in yellow and orange. The Philadelphia *Still Life: Vase with Sunflowers* also employs a pale blue background. In some of the *Sunflower* paintings, van Gogh moves in much closer: the *Still Life: Vase with Sunflowers* (lost in the Second World War) concentrates on the heads of the flowers only. *Three Sunflowers in a Vase* (private collection) also focuses on the enormous heads of the sunflowers.

The flowerpieces painted in 1887 with the pale blue vase are particularly zesty with colour: yellows, whites, reds, blues, browns vie for superiority (*Vase with Daisies and Anemones*, O). In the Geneva *Vase with Lilacs, Daisies and Anemones* Vincent van Gogh shows what a talent he had for composing with colour: though the blue vase is central, as is usual with most of van Gogh's flowerpieces, the yellow daisies are set on the extreme left of the painting. The blues of the lilacs and anemones take up most of the space of the painting, complemented by the pale blue background (so like a sky) and the sonorous blue of the vase. However, the yellow of the daisies dominates the painting, but is kept in check by their position on the left. The combination of the large areas of the blues of the flowers, vase and background and the small area of yellow daisies makes for a superb harmony of colour.

The flowerpieces had to be painted swiftly, as van Gogh explained in a letter to his brother: 'I am working at it every morning from sunrise on, for the flowers fade too soon, and the thing is to do the whole in one rush.' (no. 526) *Majolica Jar with Branches of Oleander* (1888, Metropolitan Museum, New York) again employs a relatively 'static' background (lime green wall and yellow table), with the blooms again being the subject of the painting. The colours of the leaves and setting are held back, so that the pinks and reds and whites of the flowers stand out all the more.

Some of van Gogh's flowerpieces are overwhelmingly brilliant in hue: *Vase with Daisies and Anemones* (1887, O) is one of these ultra-radiant paintings, with reds, oranges, yellows, whites, purples and blues all vieing for attention. The sense of amazement which the colourful flowers seems to instil in the painter is carried over into the background, which's not the uni-form colour of later flowerpieces (such as the *Sunflower* series) but a dense pattern of white, red, yellow and green dabs of paint. *Rosebush in Blossom* (National Museum of Western Art, Tokyo) is one of van Gogh's light, airy Nature studies. The pinky-white petals of the roses are added on last, so they look like they're floating on the surface of the canvas. Van Gogh moves close to the rosebush, so the blossoms fill up the entire painting.

Other still life paintings of roses and flowers include *Still Life: Vase with Roses* (New York) in which the vase is packed to overflowing with pink and yellow roses; *Pink Roses in a Vase* (Walter Annenberg collection) with creamy-pink petals and a bright green vase; later flowerpieces such as *Red Poppies and Daisies* (Buffalo),

The series of flowerpieces of the mid-1880s are much darker than the later paintings. In 1886 van Gogh painted pansies, chrysanthemums and peonies (O), carnations (Washington), daisies (Philadelphia), zinnias and geraniums (Ottawa), lilac (Ballwin), asters and salvia (The Hague), poppies (Hartford) and hollyhocks (Zurich). Most of these flowerpieces are seen against a dark background, often a neutral brown or grey. The space around the vases are thick with shadows. Yet, despite the gloom of the back wall and the setting, the colours of the flowers do shine forth: the deep reds of the poppies in *Vase with Poppies, Cornflowers, Peonies and Chrysanthemums* (O) and *Vase with Red Poppies* (Hartford, Connecticut), the brilliant white of the zinnias in *Vase with Zinnias and Other Flowers* (National Gallery of Canada, Ottawa).

GARDENS AND PARKS

Vincent van Gogh painted many gardens and parks. Rather than the wide view or long shot, van Gogh's gardens are often tighter views, with large parts of the landscape not shown. The canvas is tilted downwards, to capture the abundance of the earth. The famous *Irises* is one of these garden views: looking down at the soil, with the plants and flowers seen from slightly above. Even a picture such as the equally famous *Church in Auvers* (Musée d'Orsay), all gaunt angles and shadows, has a flowery mead in front of it, seen from above, dappled with white and yellow petals. Some of van Gogh's studies of gardens and nature concentrates on very small sections of the world: in *Clumps of Grass* (1889, private collection), van Gogh frames a few cluster of grass, limiting his palette to green predominantly, with white and black as the secondary hues. In *Two White Butterflies* (1889) clumps of grass are again the subject of the painting – the white butterflies are simply tiny adjuncts to another landscape study.

Pine Trees and Dandelions in the Garden of Saint-Paul Hospital (O) is another of those van Gogh paintings that tilts downward, to concentrate on grass, flowers and a few tree trunks. Van Gogh's sense of composition is again acute here, as he places two large, near-vertical trunks on the left, leaving an open space for the dandelion and grass in the centre and right.

Other paintings in which the main subject is the variety of colour in patches of grass include *Pasture in Bloom* (O), a mass of vertical brushstrokes, predominantly green, modulated by red, yellow and blue; *Couple Walking Between Rows of Trees* (Cincinnati); *Daubigny's Garden* (A); *The Grove* (New York); *Green Ears of Wheat* (Jerusalem); *Flowering Garden* (Metropolitan Museum); and *Garden Behind a House* (Kunsthaus Zurich). The drawings of parks, gardens and patches of grass reveal van Gogh's eye for building up a picture from repetitions of tiny details – petals, flowerheads, blades of grass, stalks, leaves. Drawings such as *Garden with Flowers* (1888, Winterhur) and *La Crau Seen from Montmajour* (1888, A) show the artist covering every inch of the paper with pencil and ink marks, so it looks textural, dense with varying tones and patterns. Some marks are short lines, others are close half-circles, while others are simply dots, to convey the stubble of the wheatfields.

Some of Vincent van Gogh's most restful paintings are the wide views of the countryside, such as *Harvest at La Crau, with Montmajour in the Background* (1888), one of the favourites for postcards; *View of Arles with Irises in the Foreground* (1888), with its pleasingly gentle diagonal sections of yellow flowers, green grass, and irises; *Fishing Boats on the Beach at Saintes-Maries* (1888); *The Langlois Bridge at Arles with Women*

Washing (O), *Farmhouse in Provence* (Washington), and *Public Park with Weeping Willow: The Poet's Garden I* (Chicago).

Van Gogh's *Daubigny's Garden* (collection Rudolf Staechelin, Basel) is one of his superb rectangular format compositions, depicting Nature at the height of its powers. The painting, a mass of curly, energetic brushstrokes, in the familiar van Gogh manner, with the flowerbed being especially vivaciously circumscribed. Van Gogh does not make the colours of the flowers too abundant (as he often did). Instead, he limits the palette of the painting to a few dashes of red and orange, with just one red spot in amongst the foreground flowerbed. The lack of 'warm' colour, though, does not make *Le Jardin de Daubigny* any less radiant. Van Gogh's *Daubigny's Garden* shows that even in its greens Nature is extraordinarily rich. Bright hues such as red and yellow are not required to express the sense that Nature is supremely fecund. Some of van Gogh's most satisfying paintings are those of gardens surrounded by buildings or fences, such as the radiant *Courtyard of the Hospital in Arles* (Winterhur), which's a mass of flowers and colour, or the equally profuse vegetation in the *View of Arles, Orchard in Bloom with Poplars in the Foreground* (Munich).

Van Gogh's depiction of a classic Impressionist subject, *Field with Poppies* (as found in Monet and Renoir) is another image of Paradise: it's a welter of different hues of green, with the poppies dabbed in red on top. One of the poppy paintings (The Hague) has the whole two-thirds of the composition taken up by dabs of red. Van Gogh was a master at transforming seemingly ordinary corners of the world – a patch of grass next to a field, some bushes beside a country track, a pasture in bloom, undergrowth – into something radiant. In these paintings, such as *Park at Asnières in Spring* (Singer Museum, Laren), *Banks of the Seine with Pont de Clichy in the Spring* (Dallas Museum of Fine Arts), *Path in the Woods* (A) and *Undergrowth* (Utrecht), van Gogh turns the everyday world, taken for granted by most folk, into special, incandescent spaces. Once he had the technique and vision, he could transform the everyday, even though he might have been aiming for a simple record of what was there. He could take a subject that many might not even notice, such as the *Corner of Voyer d'Argenson Park at Asnières* (private collection) or the *Banks of the Seine with Pont de Clichy in the Spring* (Dallas), and make them into magical places with their own vigorous sense of life. The banks of the Seine become a riot of white and blue flowers sprinkled on grass with waving trees above, while the corner of Voyer d'Argenson Park is vivid with white, yellow and red flowers on bright sap greens. Some of the flower and garden paintings seem impossibly paradisal and profuse with colour – such as *Flowering Garden* (Metropolitan Museum, New York), with its rows of yellow, white, red, blue and orange flowers, or *Flowering Garden with Path* (The Hague), a mass of dabs of blue, purple, red, white, yellow and green.

One cannot imagine Paris looking quite as wild and radiant now as it does in van Gogh's 1887 painting of the *Vegetable Gardens in Montmartre* (Stedelijk Museum). With short lines of red, blue, yellow, white, cerulean, green and white van Gogh depicts an expansive, lively world. One of the more subdued of van Gogh's park paintings is *Park with a Couple and a Fir Tree: The Poet's Garden III* (1888, private collection). 'Subdued', but not weak: in fact, this is one of van Gogh's most powerful compositions. 'Now imagine an immense pine tree of greenish-blue,' van Gogh wrote to Theo, 'spreading its branches horizontally over a bright green lawn, and gravel splashed with light and shade. Two figures of lovers in the shade of the great tree: size 30 canvas' (no. 552). First of all, van Gogh uses the dynamism of the diagonal (of the path). Next, he divides the painting into three main areas: the path, the grass, and the tree. Thirdly, he has the dark tone of the tree set above the light tones of the path (most landscape paintings have light over dark as their fundamental tonal element). Having the dark tree above the light path creates the tension in the painting: the tree is so vast, it overshadows the couple and the park. The painting is thus a study of shadows (like so many landscape paintings). Fourth, van Gogh severely limits his palette. No red or yellow flowers here, no warm hues at all (except for a few dabs of red in the flower border behind the couple). There are two dominant colours in *Park with a Couple and Fir Tree*: the cream-grey of the path, and the green of the grass and tree. What is striking about the painting is the colour of the fir tree: van Gogh has depicted it with dense, green-blue and black hues. His ubiquitous short, straight brushstrokes are wholly in tune with the reality of the fir leaves and branches. Van Gogh has caught the presence of a fir tree skillfully and poetically: the way it looms over the park and the couple passing beneath it, but also the beauty of its leaves. The fir tree is not regarded as innately 'beautiful', like cherry or apple trees in blossom, but van Gogh shows that even the angular, sombre-hued fir can be magical.

Other pictures related to *Park with a Couple and Fir Tree* include *A Lane in the Public Garden at Arles* (O) in which the few human figures are dominated by the trees; in the centre of the painting is another dark fir tree. In *Entrance to the Public Park at Arles* (Washington), trees are again predominant, but the dusty yellow path breaks up the composition, leading the eye into the park. In *The Lovers: The Poet's Garden IV* (whereabouts unknown) the couple are central, in the foreground, the line of trees behind them enhancing their walk with curling forms that look like flames. *The Public Park at Arles* (private collection) is again laid out along the diagonal with one solitary figure on the extreme right. In this painting, the fir trees are overarched by the autumnal colours of other trees. In *Couples in the Voyer d'Argenson Park at Asnières* (1887), van Gogh depicts a subdued grey sky above an orchard, recalling his later olive grove paintings.

Vincent van Gogh

SKIES

When good old Corot said a few days before his death – "last night in a dream I saw landscapes with skies all pink," well, haven't they come, those skies all pink, and yellow and green into the bargain, in the impressionist landscapes? All of which means that there are things one feels coming, and they are coming in very truth.

Vincent van Gogh, letter (no. 489)

Van Gogh's skies are some of his most accomplished works. Like many an artist before him and after him, van Gogh lost himself in the endless, essentially abstract spaces of the sky. Celestial events such as clouds or stars did not have to be rendered with a realistic precision. The artist was free, in other words, to dream.

In a letter (no. 543) Vincent van Gogh describes one of the *Starry Sky* paintings:

The sky is greenish-blue, the water royal blue, the ground mauve. The town is blue and violet, the gas is yellow and the reflections are russet-gold down to greenish-bronze. On the blue-green expanse of sky the Great Bear sparkles green and pink, its discreet pallor contrasts with the harsh gold of the gas.

Starry Night Over the Rhone (September 1888, Musée d'Orsay) is one of van Gogh's more expansive landscapes, suffused with dark ultramarine and greens. The Great Bear constellation is extraordinarily vast, more like a Hollywood backdrop than a real sky. *Starry Night Over the Rhone* recalls Whistler's *Nocturnes*: the painting's pictorial space is flat and awash with colour, like Whistler's images. it is a hymn to the beauty of light at night, a simple but ever-recurring phenomena. At this moment there must be someone somewhere on the planet gazing at lights flickering at night. Van Gogh takes this 'ordinary' subject and makes it extraordinary. *Starry Night Over the Rhone* becomes a pæan to nocturnal luminescence.

Vincent van Gogh was 'enormously' interested, he said, in tackling the 'problem of painting night scenes and effects on the spot' (no. 537). Of his *Starry Sky* series of paintings, van Gogh wrote:

> ...when shall I paint my *starry sky*, that picture which preoccupies me continuously? Alas! Alas! it is just as our excellent colleague Cyprien says in J.-K. Huysmans' *En Ménage*: "The most beautiful pictures are those one dreams about when smoking pipes in bed, but one will never paint." (B 7)

Of course, Vincent van Gogh *did* get to paint his *Starry Sky*. In fact, it turned out to be one of his most celebrated images. The New York *Starry Sky* (June 1889, Museum of Modern Art) is a mass of swirling, curling brushstrokes. Seen in a raking light the thickness of the brushstrokes becomes prominent. Van Gogh's treatment of oil paint is vigorous and self-confident here. Van Gogh enlarged the celestial objects so they were vast in the sky. Not only did he enlarge each star, van Gogh also encircled them with a huge white-yellow halo. Each of the eleven stars is a brilliant world, and the crescent moon, a familiar van Gogh motif, is an enormous yellow form. Even the stars above the café in *The Café Terrace on the Place du Forum, Arles, at Night* (1888, O), are given huge haloes of yellow. The most startling heavenly objects in *The Starry Sky*, though, are the two interconnecting spiral nebulæ. This is a visionary sky, where the constellations are not mere pinpricks glinting over infinite distances, to be easily ignored, but enormous, glowing presences. Van Gogh drives home the visionary aspect of the painting by his use of a vigorous impasto technique. The paint is laid on thickly and dragged into circles and spirals. Only the town below is painted with (short) straight lines: every other part of the picture, from the dark cypress to the spiral nebulæ, is delineated with curving brushstrokes. The interlinked nebulæ are the boldest element of the painting: dead centre, curling around each other, they look like a cosmic expression of the Chinese yin and yang. *The Starry Night* is a vivid manifestation of van Gogh's Biblical, dualistic vision. His paintings dramatize the interrelationship between light and dark, day and night, sun and moon, sky and land, Heaven and Earth, the human and the divine. *The Starry Sky* series are hymns to the immensity, the infinity, the ceaseless energy of the cosmos, for the lamplit towns are dominated by the ultramarine and prussian blue skies above. Even though it is nighttime (when things seem to be asleep or dormant), and the colour of the sky is blue (the most 'passive' colour), and not much seems to be happening in the sky (there's just stars there), these skies dominate intensely.

INTERIORS

Vincent van Gogh's *Bedroom* is one of his most celebrated paintings. But van Gogh did not conceive of it in the way that it is now received, as an expression of exaggerated angst. For van Gogh the *Bedroom* painting was mainly a celebration of colour. He described the painting in a letter to Theo:

> The walls are pale violet. The floor is of red tiles.
> The wood of the bed and chairs is the yellow of fresh butter, the sheets and pillows very light greenish-citron.
> The coverlet scarlet. The window green.
> The toilet table orange, the basin blue.
> The doors lilac. (no. 554)

Outdoor Café at Night, one of van Gogh's most famous images, recalls, in composition, some of Monet's, Utrillo's and Sickert's city images. What makes the painting stand out from the works of Monet, Utrillo, Sickert, Pissaro or any of the (Post-) Impressionists, are the archetypal van Gogh touches: the thick, bright paint to depict the lighted wall and awning of the café, and the equally heavy mid-orange that does for the floorboards of the terrace. The sky in *Outdoor Café at Night*, too, is very much van Gogh's own: a bright blue theatrical backdrop, with each star having a wide aura. Van Gogh's interiors are often portrayed in mainstream art criticism as the products of a neurotic perception: the paintings of van Gogh's bedroom and the night café are seen as the visual equivalent of van Gogh's increasing madness. Alienated and lonely is a typical art history description of *The Night Café*. To use the stereotypical language of art criticism, *The Night Café* (Yale) is compounded of ('lurid') red walls, ('sickly') yellow lamps emanating their pallor into the near-empty room and the ('poison') green of the billiard table. 'I have tried to express the terrible passions of humanity by means of red and green.' (no. 533) Van Gogh is seen as having captured a certain bleakness about the evenings of some locals in a café at night. This is nothing particularly new: every night there are thousands of bars and cafés the world over which are just as bleak and lonely as van Gogh's *Night Café*. Van Gogh's painting is an extremely powerful vision of nocturnal despair. It seems to be the embodiment of pallid yellow sickness, the visual equivalent of the depression suicides experience in the drab Winter months of January and February, after Christmas. The exaggerated perspective of *The Night Café* and *Van Gogh's Bedroom* adds to the sense of melancholy. The empty foreground space yawns towards the viewer, a distorted void.

Vincent van Gogh

LAST WORKS

Some of Vincent van Gogh's paintings have been associated by critics with his 'madness': *Starry Night*, with its spirals of paint surrounding each star; *Wheatfield with Crows*, with its thunderous skies and jet-black birds of omen; *The Church at Auvers*, all skewed perspectives; *Night Café*, with its 'lurid' – nay, 'sickly' – mixture of greens and reds; and of course the *Self-Portraits*. Some of these 'late, mad' works of the last two years of his life are among van Gogh's most accomplished. The ones of 1890 (mainly June and July 1890) are composed within the distinctive wide horizontal 'frieze-like' format. *Undergrowth with Two Figures* (Cincinnati) presents the dual van Gogh themes of a thickly-flowered undergrowth with a pair of walking lovers. The frieze format allows van Gogh to extend his depiction of the opulence of nature; the flowers are defined loosely, with large yellow, red and white brushstrokes. Another horizontal frieze-like composition is *Wheatfields Near Auvers* (Vienna), the poppies and daisies in the foreground give way to gently sloping fields of green and yellow. Not 'mad' at all, this picture is distinctly tranquil, as are other horizontal paintings of June-July 1890, such as *Landscape with the Château of Auvers at Sunset* (A), *Daubigny's Garden* (Hiroshima Museum of Art), *Field with Wheat Stacks* (Berne), the golden *Sheaves of Wheat* (Dallas), and the houses huddled together in *Thatched Cottages by a Hill* (Tate Gallery).

At least three of the horizontal paintings can be taken as indicating tumultuous states of mind: the celebrated *Wheatfield with Crows*, *Landscape at Auvers in the Rain* and *Wheatfield Under a Cloudy Sky*. Van Gogh's solution to the difficult problem of depicting rain, in *Landscape at Auvers in the Rain* (National Museum of Wales, Cardiff), is simply to draw his brush across the canvases loaded with black pigment. The result makes the sense of rain pre-dominant: it brings the rain right up to the frontal plane of the painting, so each stream of water seems to be directly in front of the viewer. The effect is startling: after what seemed like hundreds of years of conservatively-applied paint (disregarding exceptionally tactile artists such as Leonardo and Titian for the moment), to see a painter dragging black marks across the whole of the canvas is wonderfully fresh. The colouration, too, of *Landscape at Auvers in the Rain* is startling: not content to represent rain with grey, van Gogh, with his heightened sense of the relations between colours, uses lilac and orange in bands; grey-lilac in the sky; yellow-orange for the distant hills; the town and trees in lilac and grey; the nearer fields in orange and yellow, interspersed with green.

Another notable stormy sky is *Landscape Under a Stormy Sky* (Foundation Socindee, Vaduz), which depicts livid yellow and brown clouds sailing over a placid orchard scene. Linked with the tumult of *Wheatfield with Crows* is the looming, thundery sky of *Wheatfield Under a Cloudy Sky*. The horizontal format enables van Gogh to depict the landscape of Auvers-sur-Oise as 'big sky country' (as people call Arizona). Eighty years later, American land artists such as Walter de Maria would make artworks that celebrated the vastness of the sky (with his *Lightning Field* in the New Mexico desert, for example). *Wheatfield Under a Cloudy Sky* is supposedly the picture that van Gogh had on his easel when he killed himself. In his letters he writes:

> They are infinitely vast wheat fields beneath a dismal sky, and I have not shied away from the attempt to express sadness and extreme loneliness (no. 649)

Seeing these late paintings with their depictions of rainy, thundery skies as equivalents of Vincent van Gogh's 'madness' and looming suicide is part of the van Gogh legend. Another, purely painterly view, though, might see these skies as exciting, inspiring for a painter, more challenging, for instance, than clear blue skies. The more interesting skies in Northern Europe, for example, do not occur in Summer, but in Autumn and Winter, when the wind is strong, the weather is changeable and, importantly, there are lots of clouds about. Thus, the dark blue and purple sky in *Wheatfield Under a Cloudy Sky* can be seen as an interpretation of a particular atmospheric effect: big skies over a wide-open landscape, but not necessarily the expression of someone on the verge of insanity or suicide. Seen in this way, *Wheatfield with Crows* (A), one of the 'top five van Gogh paintings' one might say, is a depiction of a striking but not unknown phenomenon: grey-blue-black clouds low over a golden field. If one travels around with one's eyes open one will see scenes like this a few times (though perhaps not with so many crows in flight). It is not the scene itself that makes *Wheatfield with Crows* so unusual as van Gogh's aggressive treatment of the paint: the brushstrokes veer off in many diagonals, creating an uneven dynamism. The multi-directional brushstrokes prevent the paint-ing from being harmonized into tranquillity. It is a painting that will not keep still. The artistic biography of van Gogh gets in the way of the painting, though: his supposed decaying mental state literally colours the late paintings, so that *Wheatfield with Crows* has impending suicide written into it, over decades of art criticism and public veneration.

NOTES

I THE MYTH AND LEGEND OF VINCENT VAN GOGH

1. The picture that van Gogh sold, according to legend, was *L'Arlésienne (Madame Ginoux)*, in the Orsay Museum. Van Gogh told Theo that the picture had been 'slashed on in an hour' (559). If this picture was sold today, it would be worth millions of dollars: not bad for an hour's work. With irony we read van Gogh's letters, which state: 'I cannot help it that my pictures do not sell. Nevertheless the time will come when people will see that they are worth more than the price of the paint' (557).

2. Henry Miller, *The Waters Reglitterized*, in *The Henry Miller Reader*, Pan 1985, 312

3. Miller: *The Time of the Assassins: A Study of Rimbaud*, New Directions, New York 1962, 60

4. Gwyneth Roberts: "Ornaments as Cultural Status Markers", in Gary Day: *Readings in Popular Culture*, Macmillan 1990, 44

5. Anthony Crabbe: "Museums of Fine And their Public", in Day, 1990, 209

II THE PSYCHOLOGY OF THE ARTIST

1. L. Durrell: *Collected Poems*, Faber 1980, 338

III THE ART OF VAN GOGH

1. See Suzanne Munich: "N.Y. Art Auction Scene: A Still Life", *Los Angeles Times*, 17 November 1990, F1, 11

2. Peter Fuller: "British Romantic Landscape Painting from Turner to Maggi Hambling", lecture, 1990, in Fuller 1993, 28

3. Martin Heidegger; *Poetry, Language, Thought*, tr. Albert Hofstater, Harper & Row, New York 1971, 32f

4. Peter Fuller: "British Romantic Landscape Painting from

Turner to Maggi Hambling", ib., 22

5. Wassily Kandinsky: "On the Problem of Form", *Der Blaue Reiter*, R. Piper, Munich 1912, and in Chipp, 162

6. Brancusi, in "Propos de Brancusi", *Prisme des Arts*, Paris, no. 12, May 1957, 6

7. in Philip James & Henry Moore: *Henry Moore on Sculpture*, Viking Press, New York 1971, 60

8. Dorothy Adlow: "Brancusi", *Drawing and Design*, 2 Feb 1927, 37f

9. Rilke, letter to 'une amie', 3, February 1923, quoted in *The Selected Poems of Rainer Maria Rilke*, tr Stephen Mitchell, Picador, 1987, 299

10. Rilke: *The Rodin-Book*, tr G. Craig Houston, Quartet 1986, 46

11. Rilke: *New Poems*, tr J.B. Leishman, Hogarth Press 1963, 57

12. Suzuki: *The Basics of Buddhist Philosophy*, Allen & Unwin 1957, quoted in Richard Woods, ed, *Understanding Mysticism*, Athlone Press 1980, 126

13. quoted in *Brancusi*, catalogue, Brummer Gallery, New York 1926

14. Beckmann, lecture, 1938, quoted in Chipp,188

15. Beckmann: "On My Painting", op.cit., in Chipp, 188

16. Kokoschka: "On the Nature of Visions", tr Heidi Medlinger & John Thwaites, in Edith Hoffman: *Kokoschka: Life and Work*, Faber 1947, 285f

17. Paul Klee: *Credo*, in *The Inward Vision: Watercolours, Drawings and Writings by Paul Klee*, Abrams, New York 1959, 5

18. Long: *Five, six, pick up sticks / Seven, eight, lay them straight*, 1980, Anthony d'Offay Gallery, September 1980

19. see Anne Seymour: "El Estanque de Basho – una nueva perspectiva", in *Piedras Richard Long*, Ministerio de Cultura, Direción general de Bellas Artes y Archivos and the British Council 1986

20. Long, quoted in Lucie-Smith: *Sculpture Since 1945*, 121

21. Durrell: *Livia*, Faber 1978, 245

BIBLIOGRAPHY

By and about Vincent van Gogh

A. Artaud: *Van Gogh, le suicidé dela societé*, Paris, 1947

K. Batt: *Die Farbenlehre van Goghs*, Cologne 1961

P. Cabanne: *Van Gogh: l'homme et son œuvre*, Editions Aimery Somogny, Paris 1961

Charles Chetham: *The Role of Vincent van Gogh's Copies in the Development of His Art*, New York 1976

P. Courthion: *Van Gogh raconté par lui-même et par ses aimis, ses contemporains, sa posterité*, Pierre Cailler, Geneva 1947

J.B. de la Faille: *The Works of Vincent van Gogh: His Paintings and Drawings*, Weidenfeld & Nicolson 1970

Vincent van Gogh: *The Complete Letters of Vincent van Gogh*, Thames & Hudson 1958

—*Verzamelde Brieven van Vincent van Gogh*, Amsterdam 1952-4

—*Letters From Provence*, ed Martin Bailey, Collins & Brown 1992

—*Van Gogh door Van Gogh: De brieven als commentaar op zijn werk*, ed Jan Hulsker, Meulenhoff, Amsterdam 1973

A.M. Hammacher: *Vincent Van Gogh*, Becht, Amsterdam 1948

—& Renilde Hammacher: *Van Gogh: A Documentary Biography*, Thames & Hudson 1982

Jan Hulsker: *The Complete van Gogh*, Phaidon 1980

—ed: *Vincent*, I & II, Summer/ Autumn 1972

R. Huyghe: *Van Gogh*, Flammarion, Paris, 1958

Jacques Lassaigne: *Vincent van Gogh*, Cassell 1988

J. Leymarie: *Van Gogh*, Pierre Tisné, Paris 1951

Melissa McQuillan: *Vincent van Gogh*, Thames & Hudson 1989

Carl Nordenfalk: *The Life and Work of van Gogh*, Philosophical Society, 1953

H. Perruchot: *La vie de van Gogh*, Hachette, Paris 1955

Ronald Pickvance: *Van Gogh in Arles*, Abrams, New York 1984

—*Van Gogh in Saint-Rémy and Auvers*, Abrams, New York 1986

Griselda Pollock & Fred Orton: *Vincent van Gogh: Artist of His Time*, Oxford 1978

John Rewald: *Post-Impressionism from Van Gogh to Gauguin*, Secker & Warburg 1978

M. Roskill: *Van Gogh, Gauguin, and the Impressionist Circle*, London, 1970

Judy Sand: "Women and Books in the Art of van Gogh", *Art History*, 11, 2, June 1988

W. Scherjon & J. de Gruyter: *Vincent van Gogh's Great Period: Arles, Saint-Rémy and Auvers-sur-Oise*, Amsterdam, 1937

Meyer Shapiro: *Vincent van Gogh*, Abrams, New York, 1950

Susan Alyson Stein, ed: *Vincent van Gogh: A Retrospective*, New York 1986

Mark Tralbaut: *Vincent van Gogh*, Chartwell Books 1969

—*Van Goghiana*, 1953-75

Evert van Uitert: *Van Gogh: Drawings*, Thames & Hudson 1979

—"Vincent's Original Contribution", *Simiolus*, 11, 1980

M. Valsecchi: *Van Gogh*, Milan 1957

John Walker: *Van Gogh Studies*, London 1981

Ingo F. Walther: *Vincent van Gogh 1853-1890: Vision and Reality*, Benedikt Taschen 1990

–& Rainer Metzger: *Vincent van Gogh: The Complete Paintings*, Taschen 1993

Bogomila Welsh-Ovcharov: *Vincent van Gogh: His Paris Period 1886-1888*, The Hague 1976

Johannes Van Der Wolk: *The Seven Sketchbooks of Vincent van Gogh*, Thames & Hudson 1987

Carol M. Zemel: *The Formation of a Legend: Vincent van Gogh*, Ann Arbor, Michigan 1980

—"Sorrowing Women, Rescuing Men: van Gogh's Images of Women and Family", *Art History*, X, 3, September 1987

Other sources

Mircea Eliade: *Ordeal by Labyrinth*, University of Chicago Press 1984

C.G. Jung: *Memories, Dreams, Reflections*, Collins 1967

Julia Kristeva: *The Kristeva Reader*, ed Toril Moi, Blackwell 1986

—*Desire in Language: A Semiotic Approach to Literature and Art*, ed Leon Roudiez, tr Thomas Gora, Alice Jardine & Leon Roudiez, Blackwell 1982

Vincent van Gogh

Rainer Maria Rilke: *Letters on Cézanne*, ed. Clara Rilke, Cape, 1988

Charles A. Riley, *Color Codes: Modern Theories of Color in Philosophy, Painting and Architecture, Literature, Music, and Psychology*, New England University Press, Hanover 1995

Harold Rosenberg, *The Tradition of the New*, Da Capo Press, New York, 1994

—*The De-Definition of Art*, University of Chicago Press 1972

ILLUSTRATIONS

Illustrations

Vincent van Gogh

1. *Peasant Man and Woman*, 1885, Zurich.
2. *The Seine With the Pont de la Grand Jatte*, 1887, Amsterdam.
3. *Peach Tree In Bloom*, 1888, Otterlo.
4. *Café Terrace At Night*, 1888, Otterlo.
5. *Park With a Couple and a Blue Fir Tree*, 1888, private collection.
6. *Self-Portrait With Bandaged Ear*, 1889, London.
7. *View of Arlès, Orchard In Bloom*, 1889, Munich.
8. *The Church At Auvers*, 1890, Paris.
9. *Wheat Fields With Cypress*, 1889, Prague.
10. *Wheat Fields With Cypresses*, 1889, Zurich.
11. *Olive Trees*, 1889, Otterlo.
12. *The Starry Night*, 1889, New York City.
13. *Bedroom At Arlès*, 1889, Chicago.
14. *Road With Man Walking, Carriage, Cypress, Star and Crescent Moon*, 1890, Otterlo.
15. *Cedar Tree With Figures*, 1888, Otterlo.
16. *Poppy Field*, Otterlo.
17. *Fir Trees At Sunset*, 1889, Otterlo.
18. *Trees*, Otterlo.
19. *Still-Life*, Otterlo.
20. *Terrace of the Café La Guinguette*, 1886, Otterlo.
21 *Wheat Field With Crows*, 1890, Amsterdam.

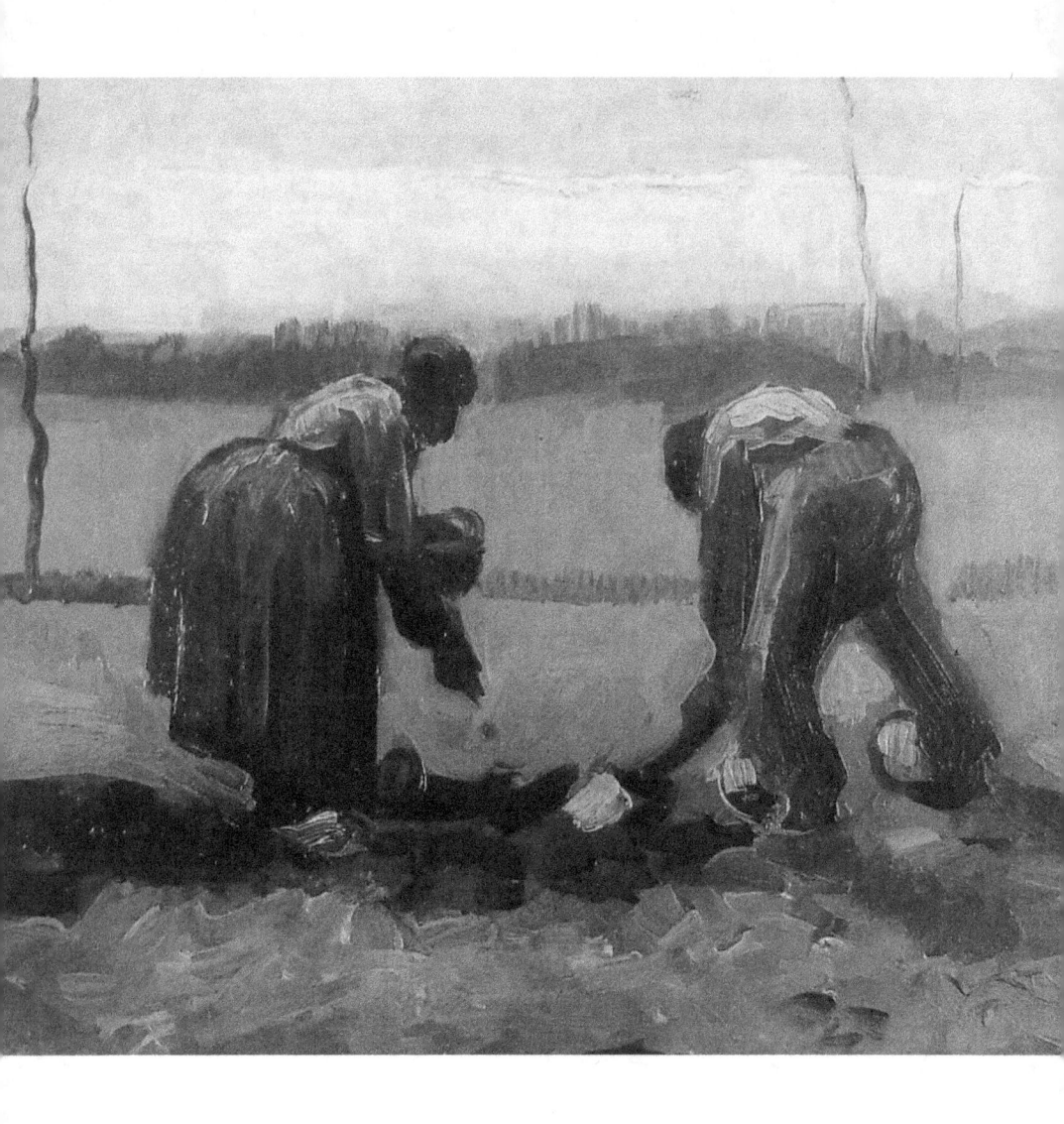

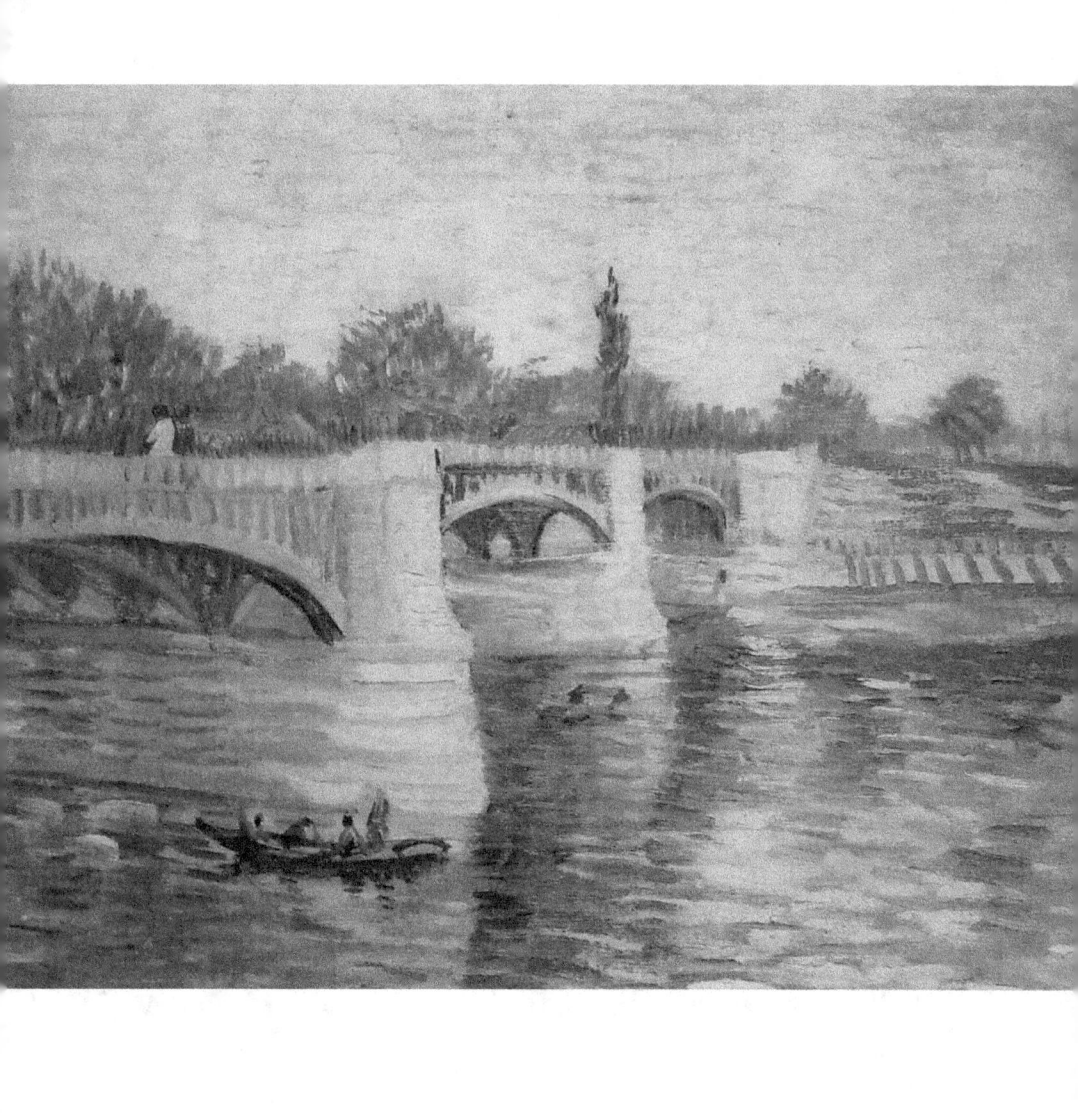

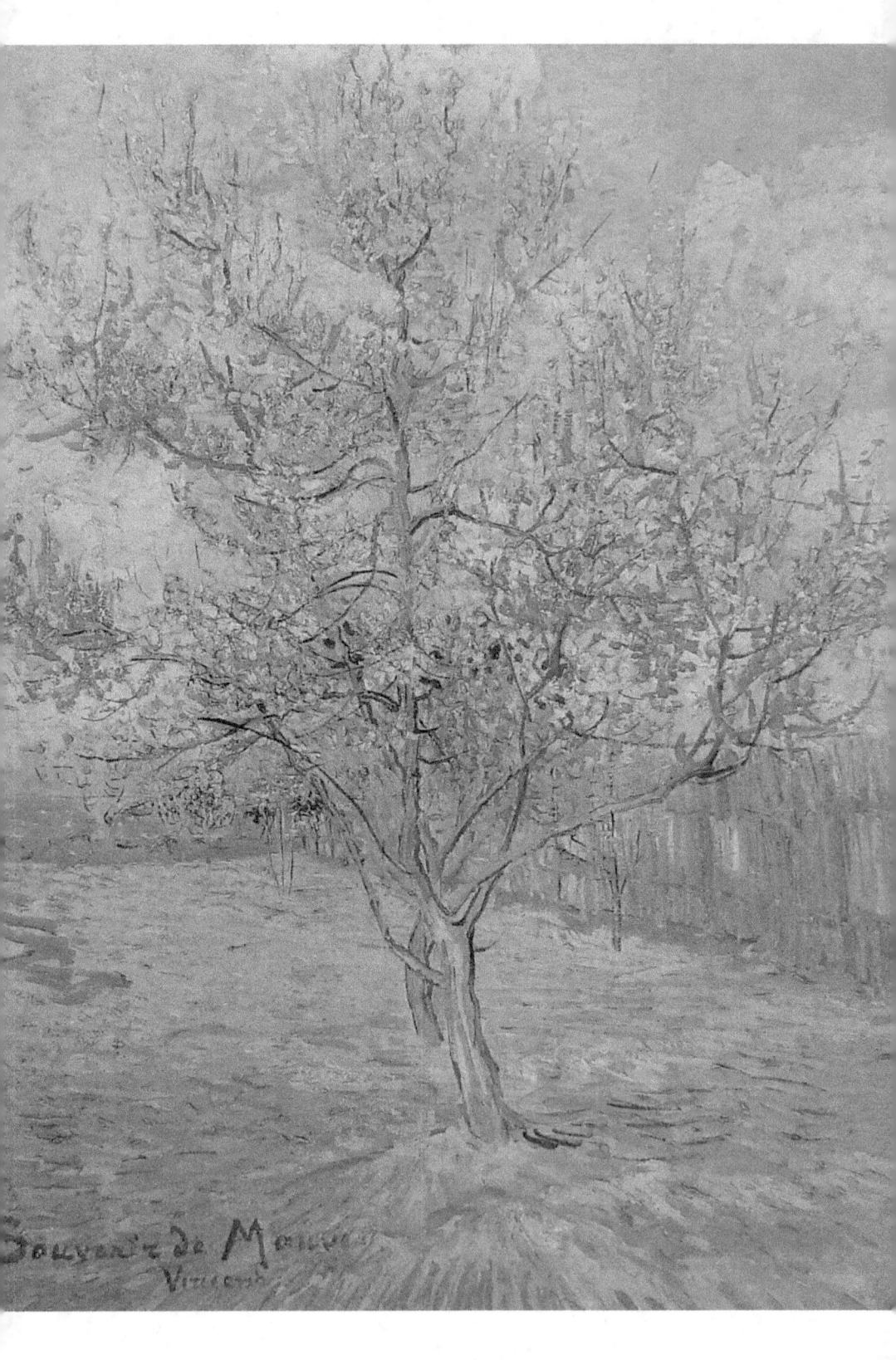

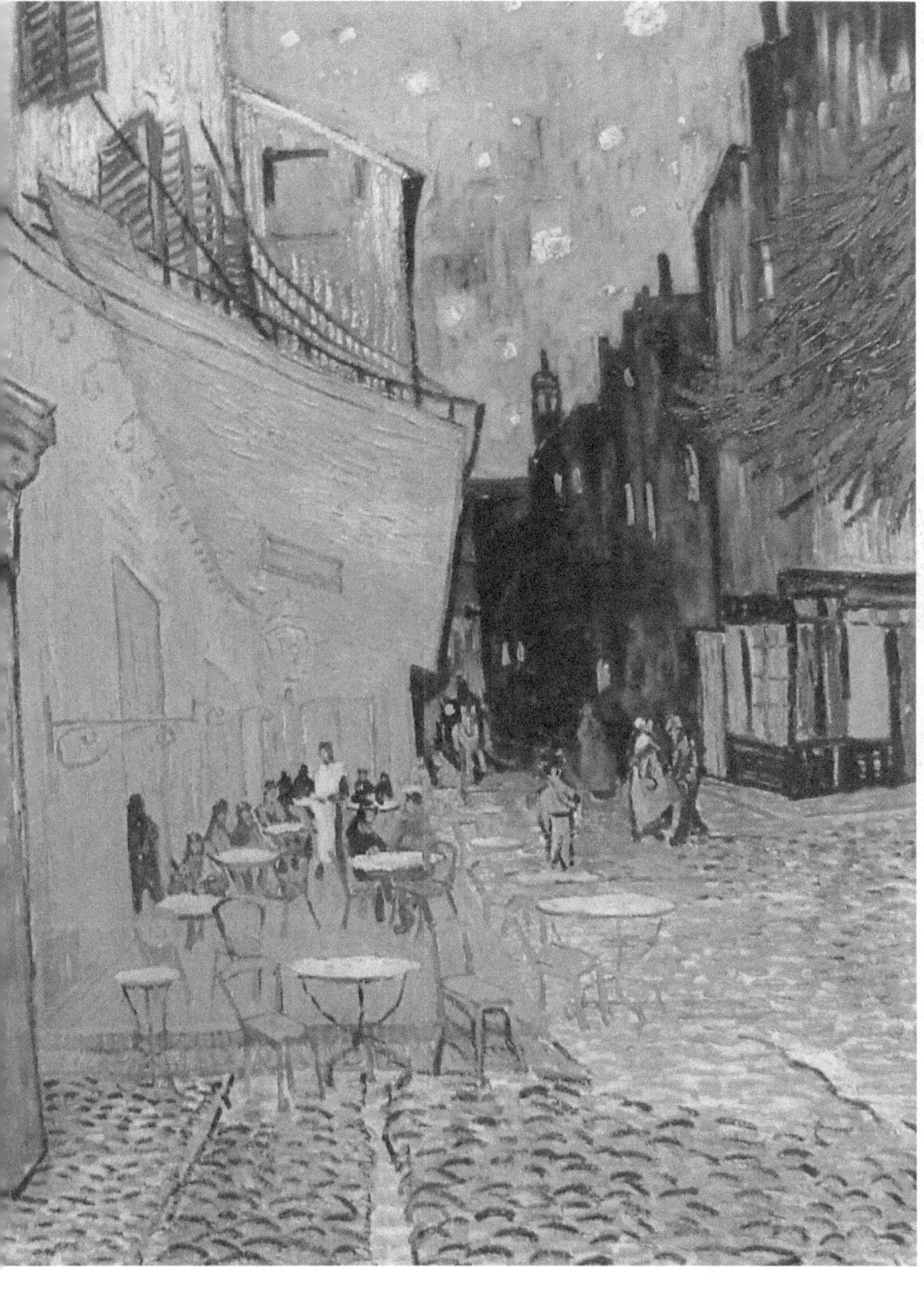

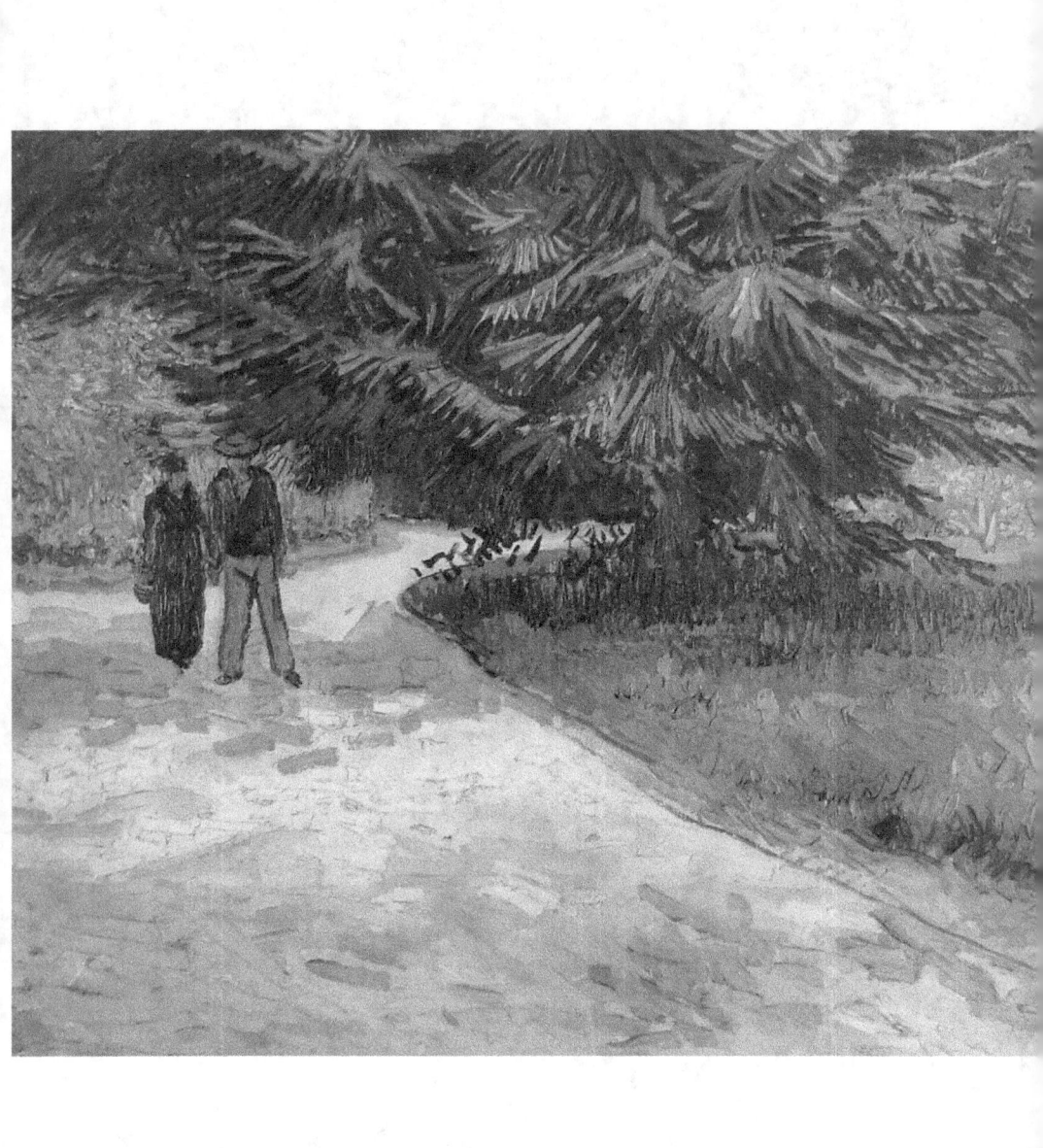

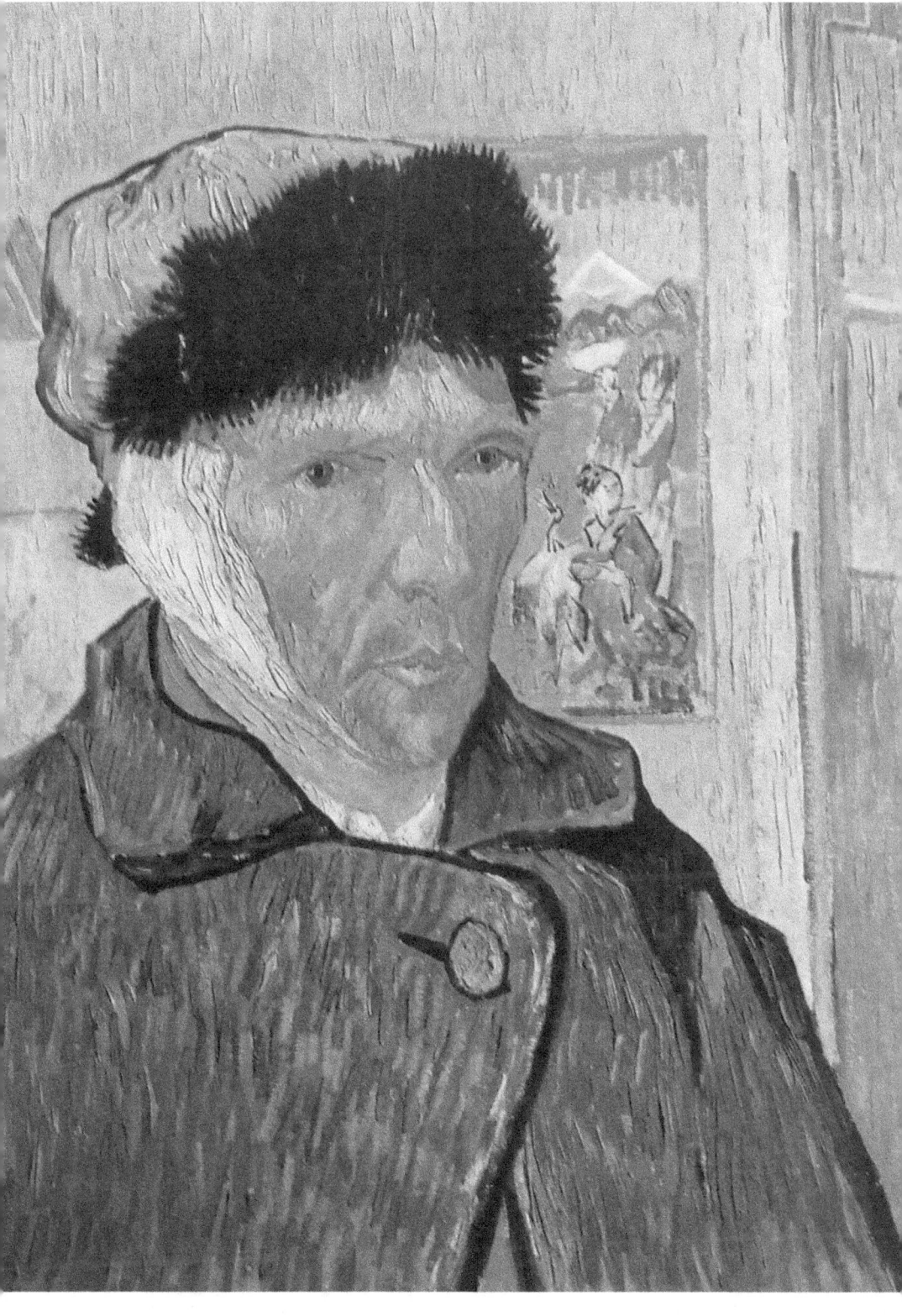

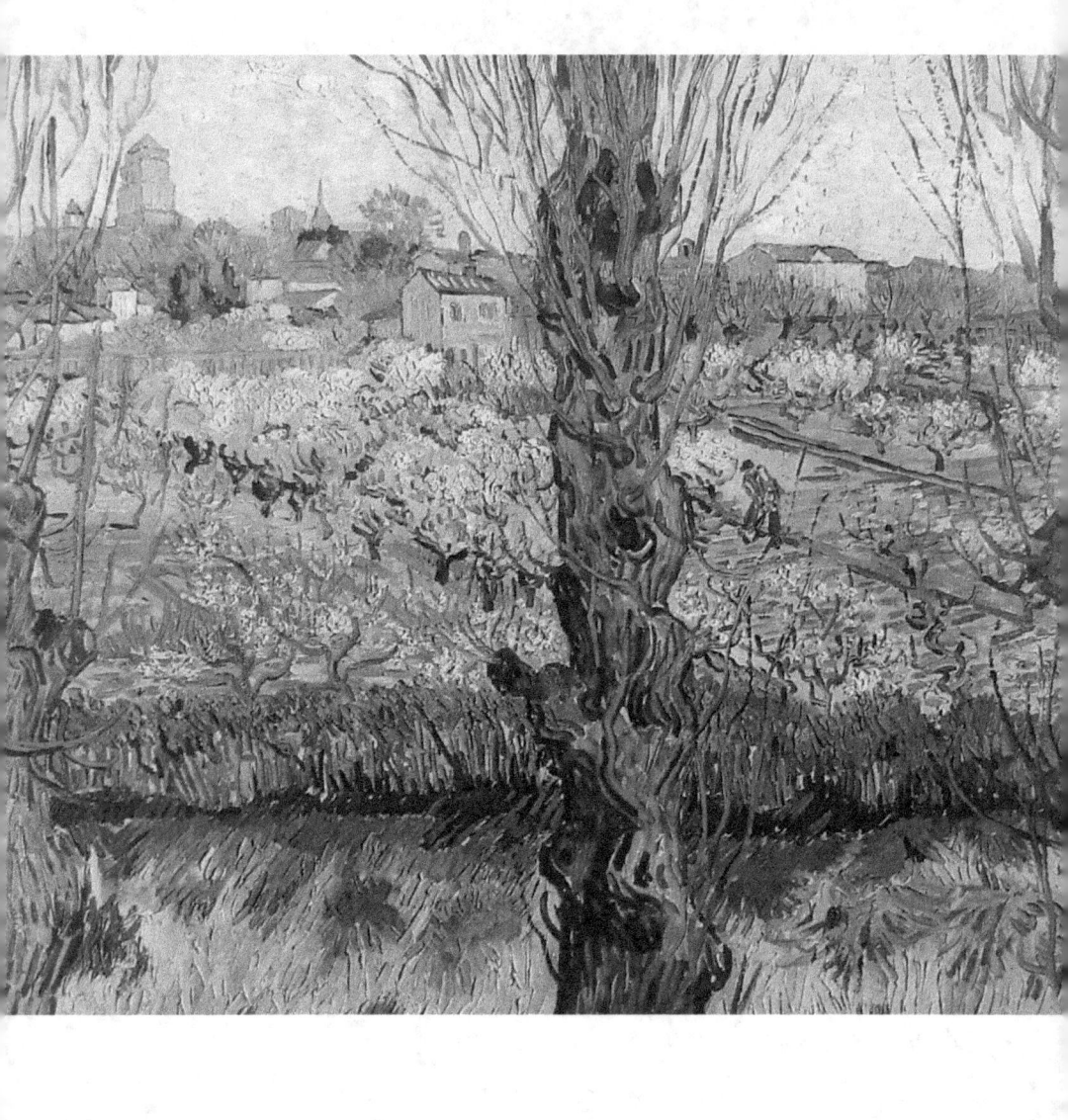

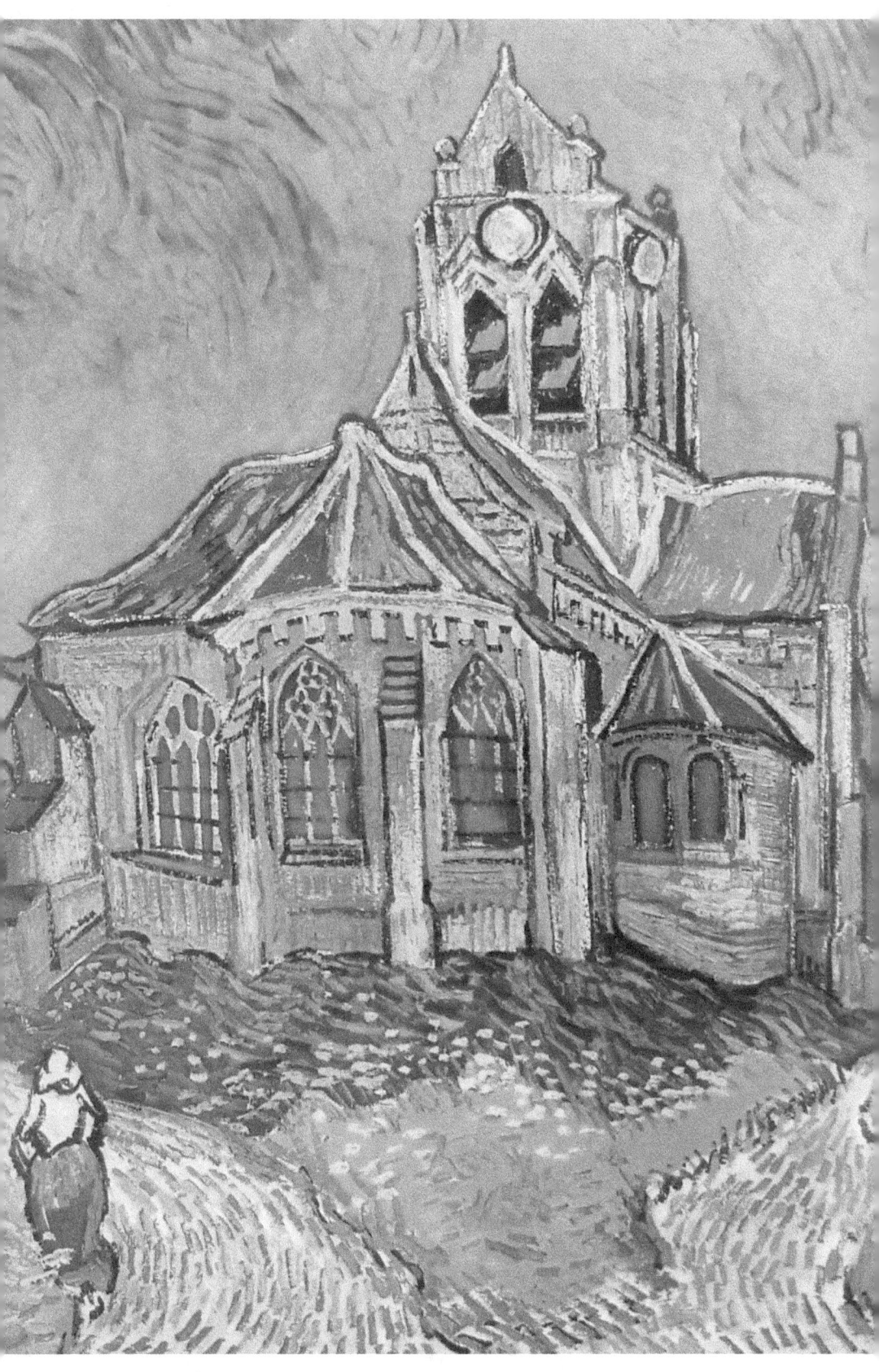

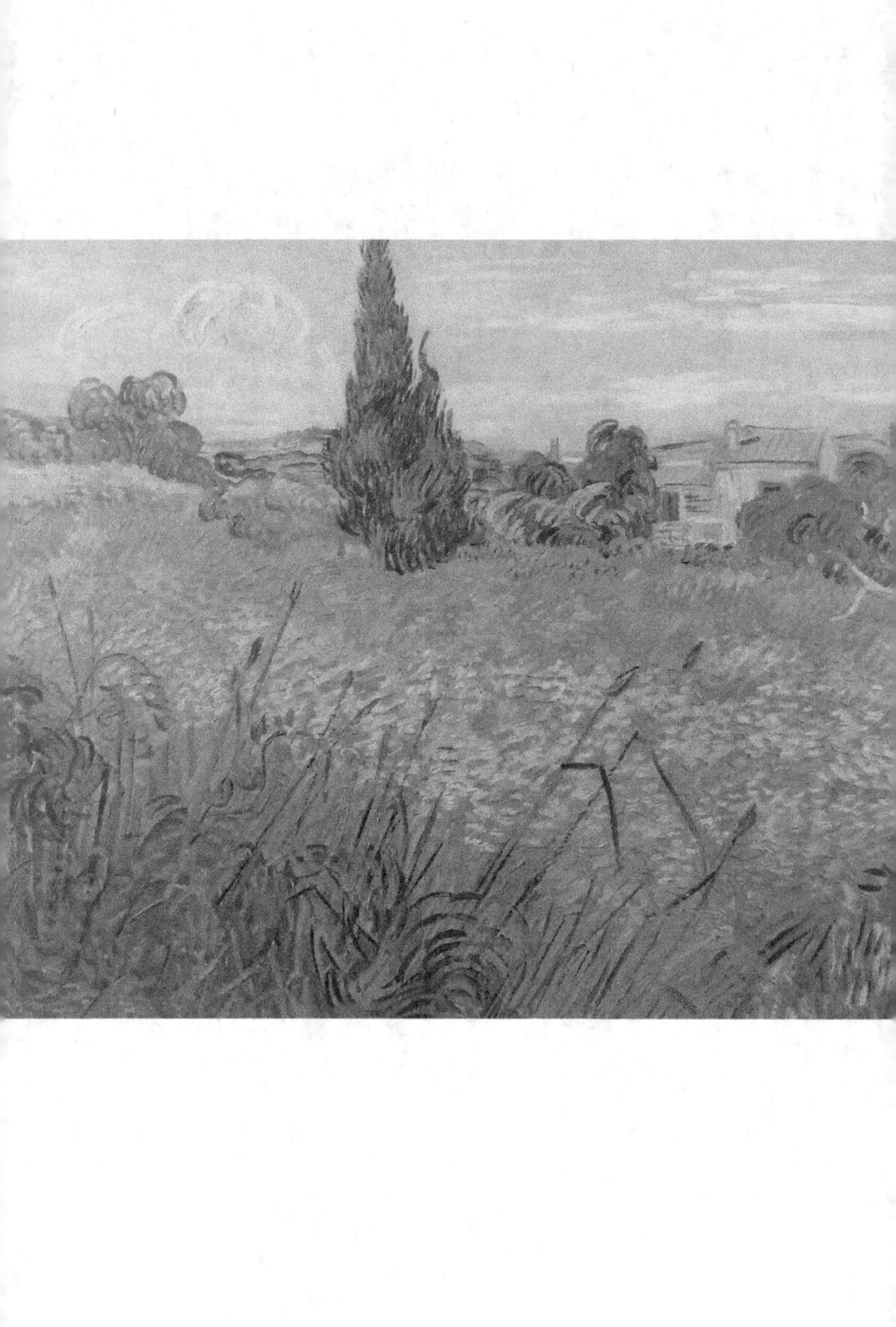

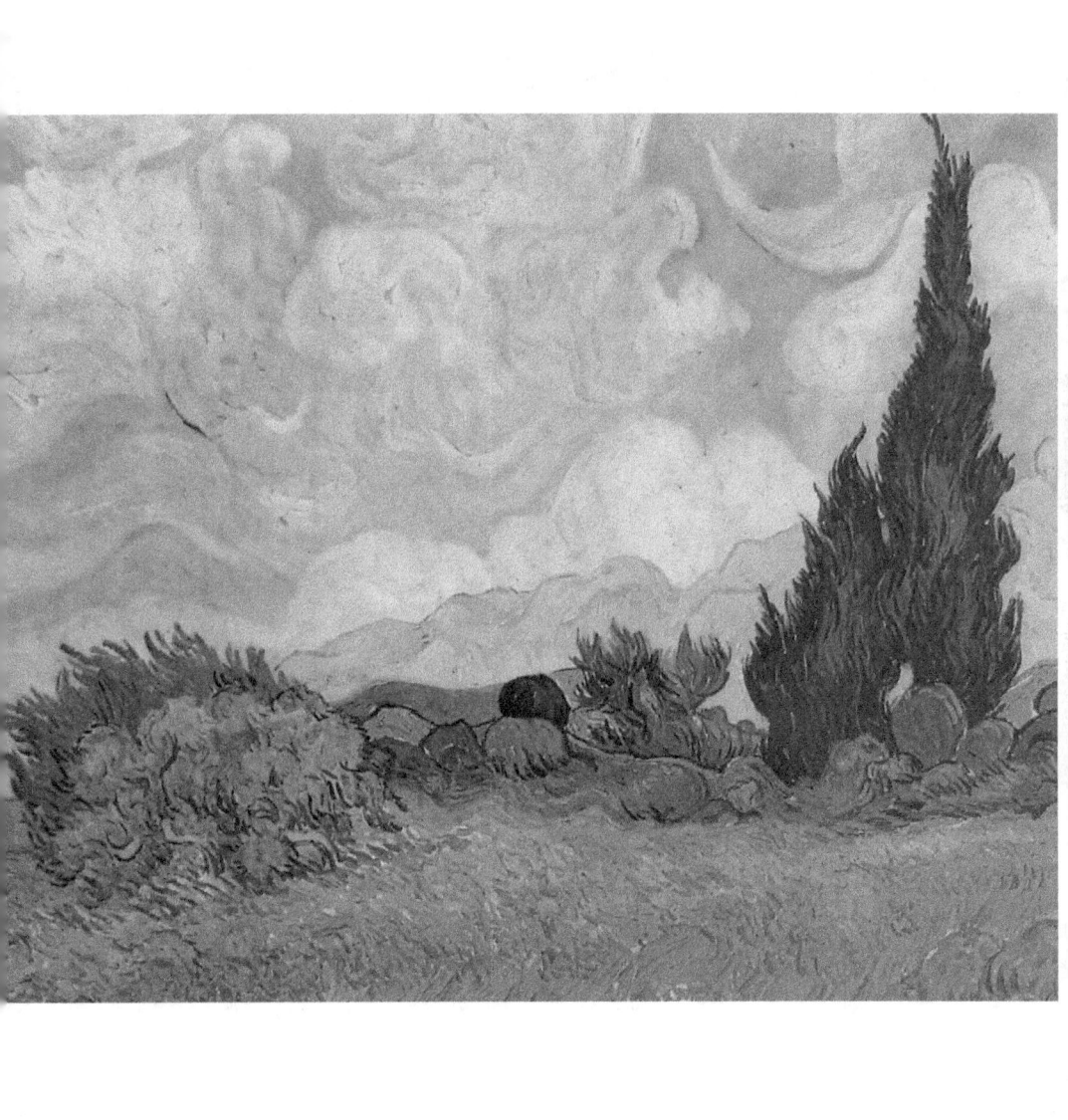

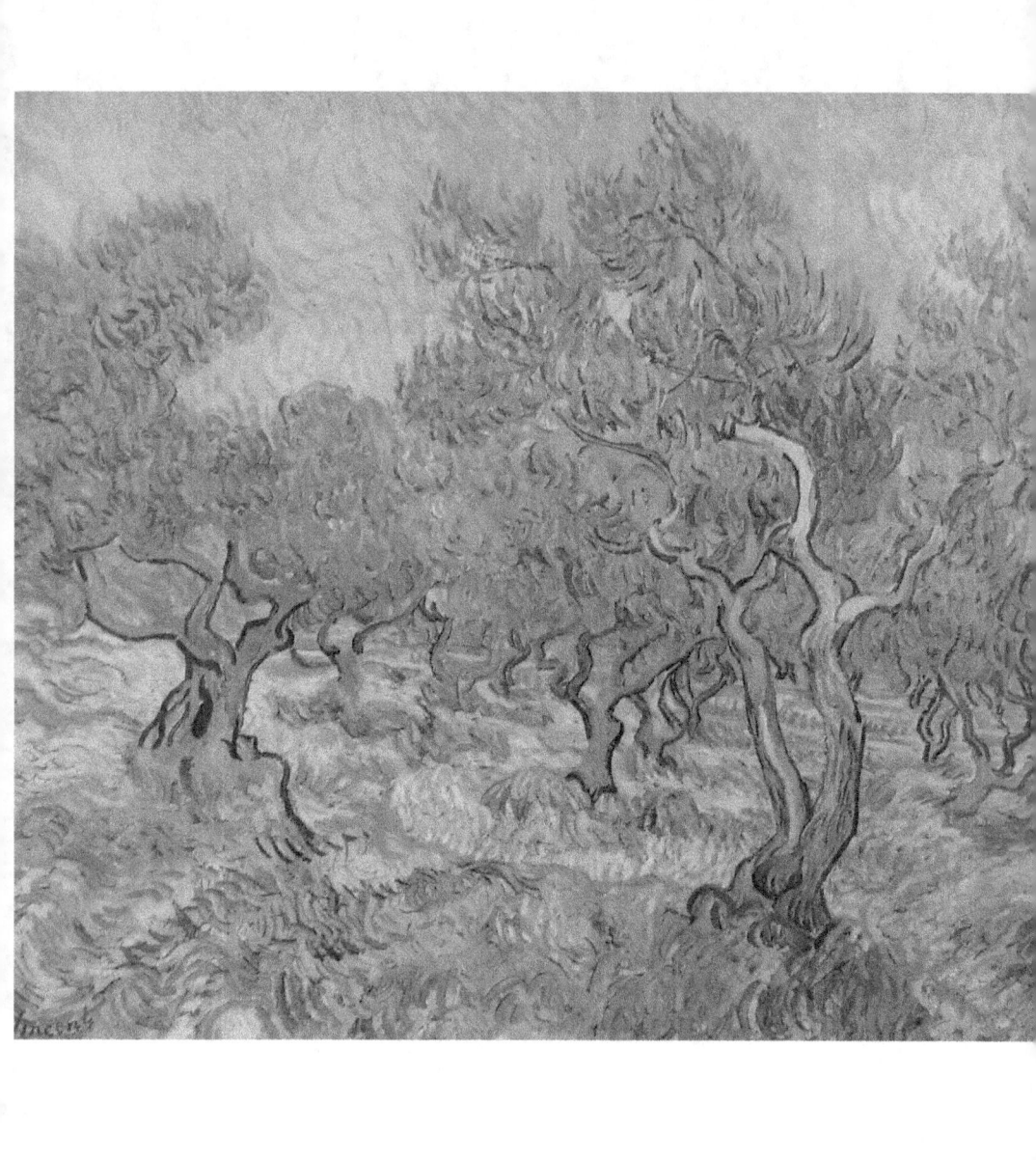

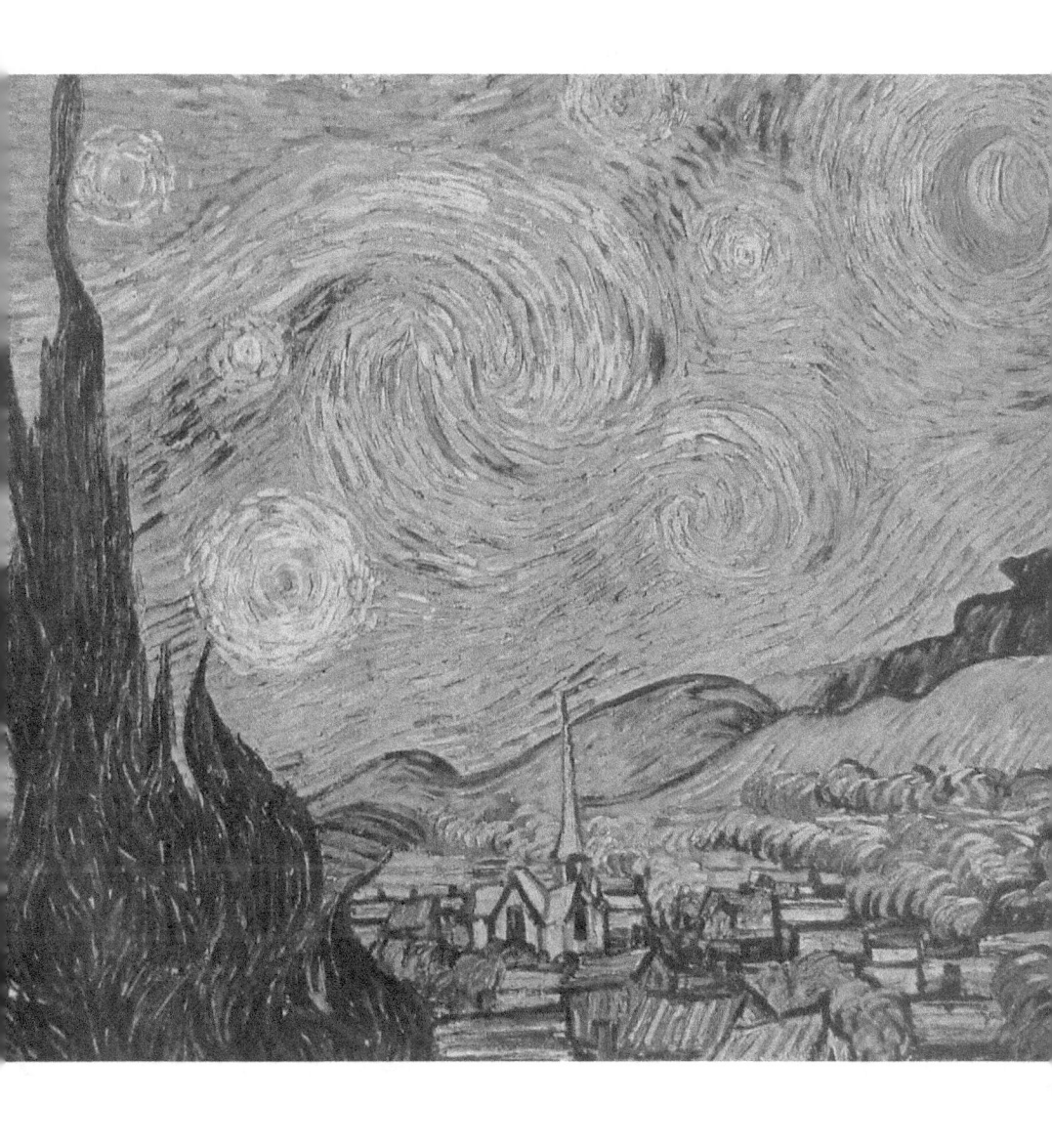

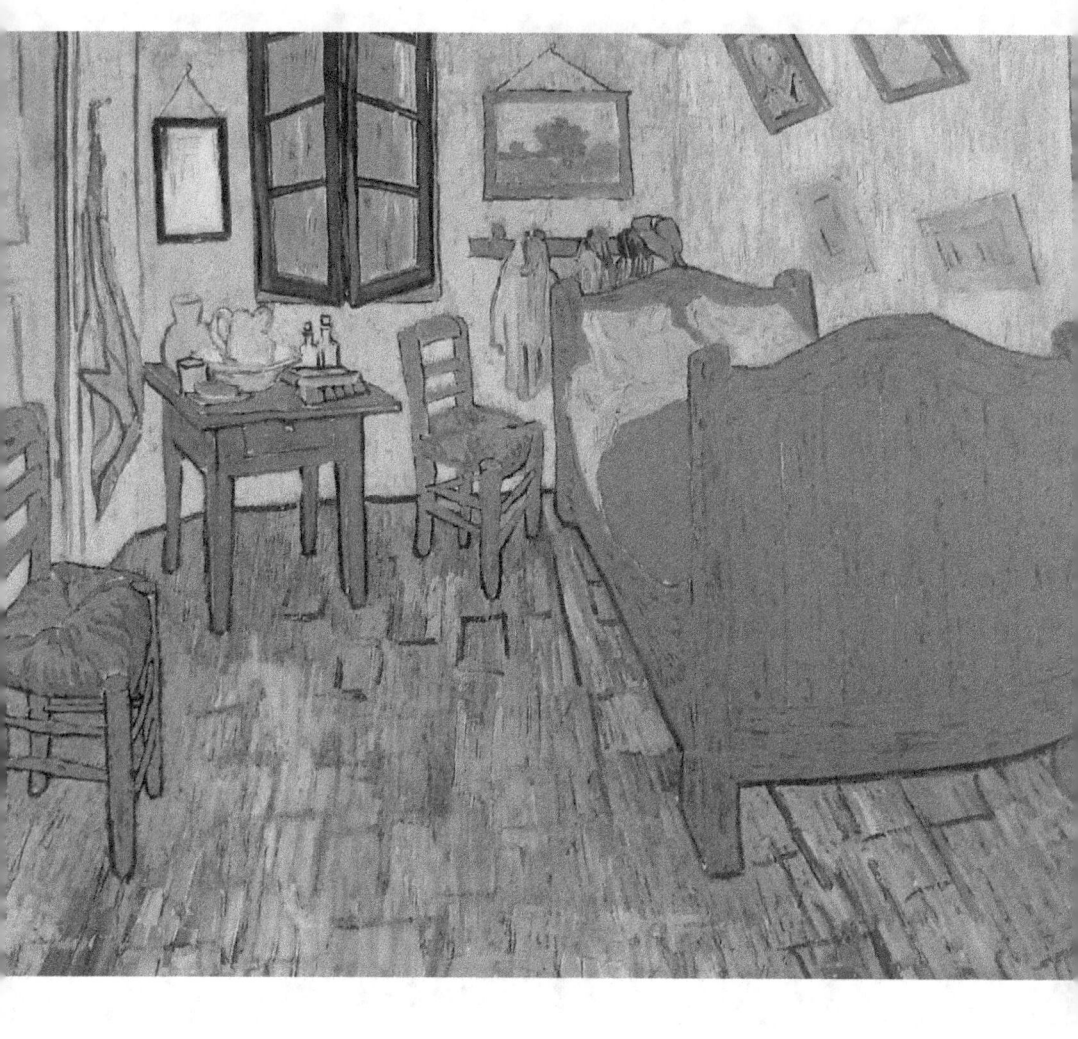

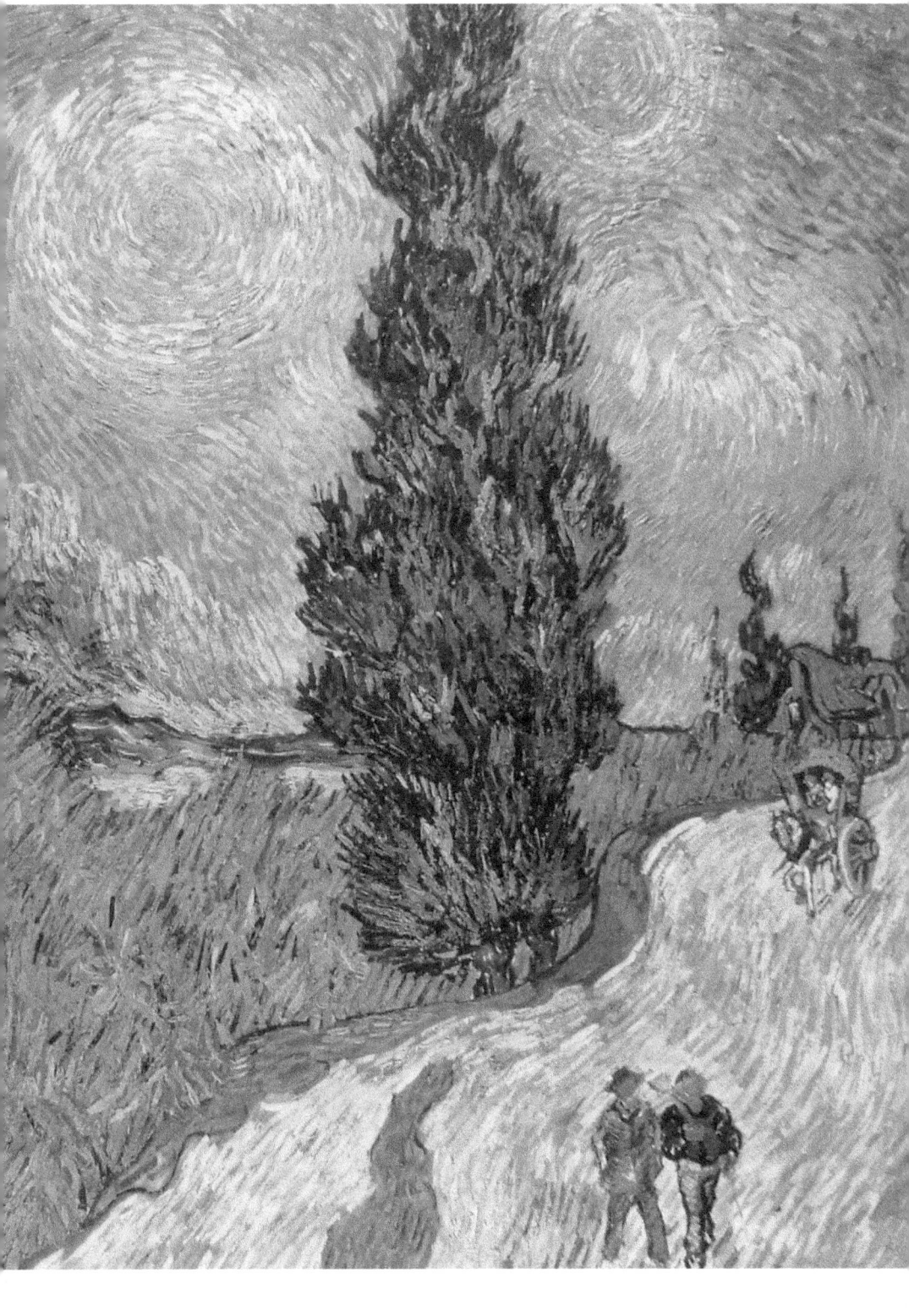

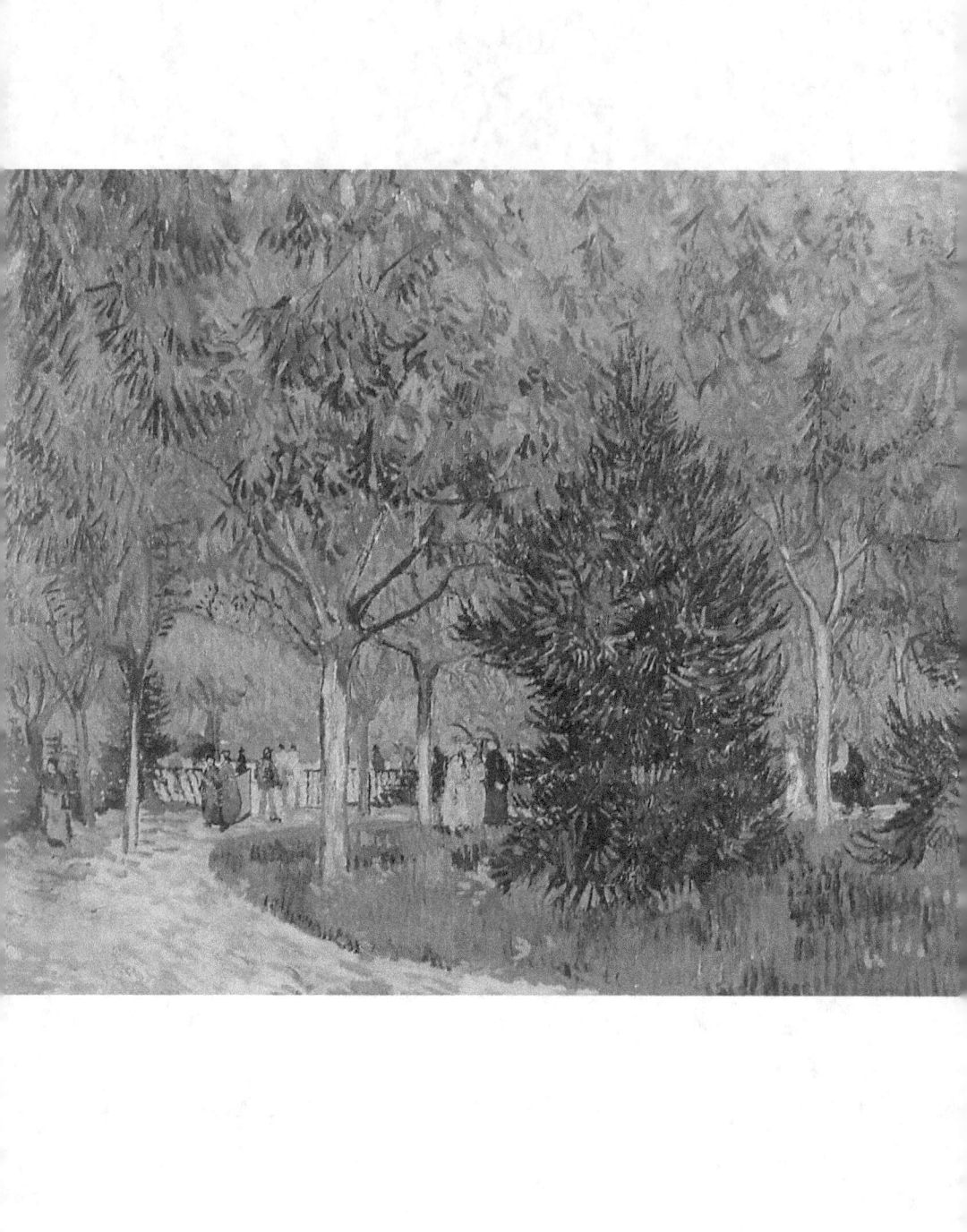

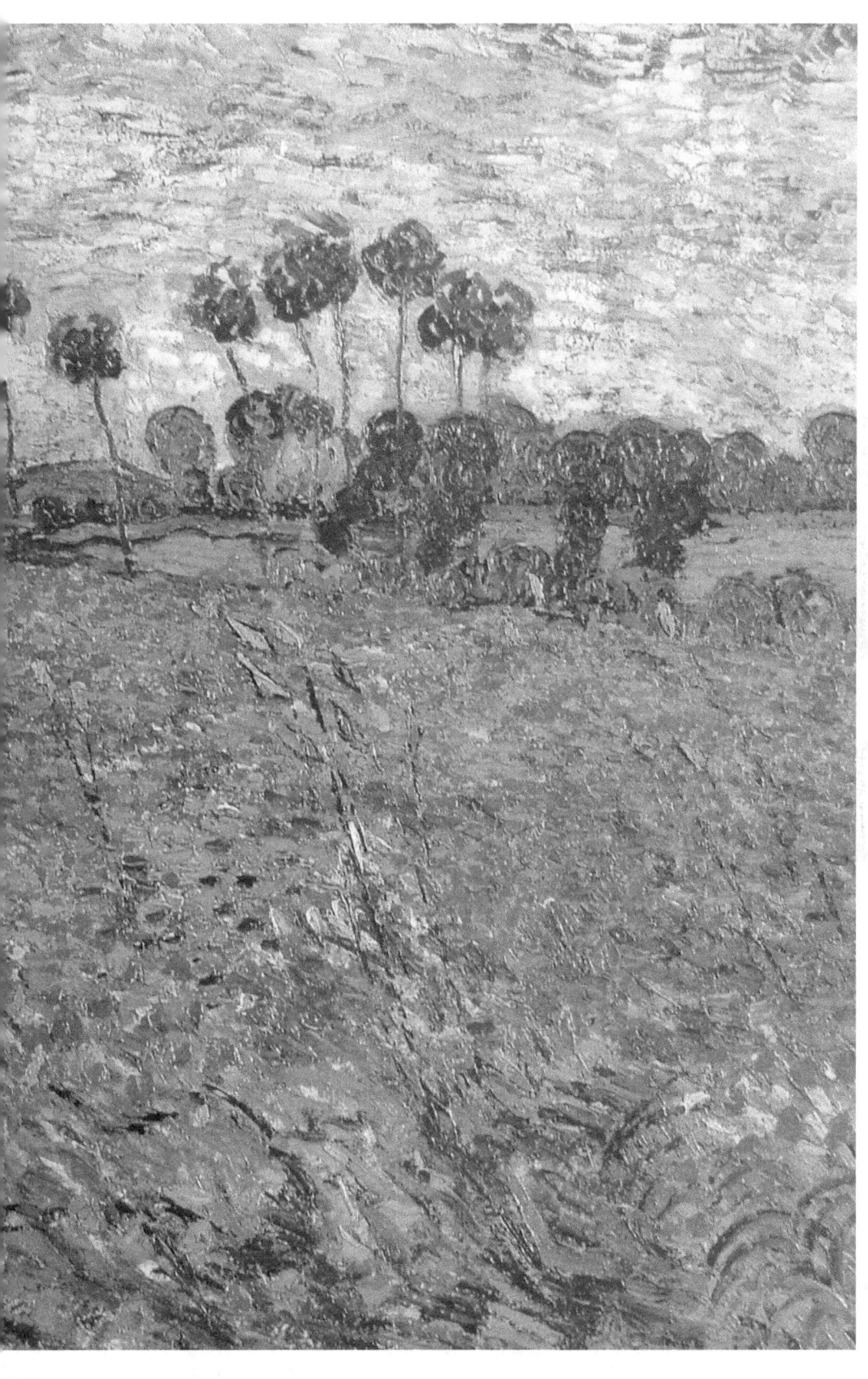

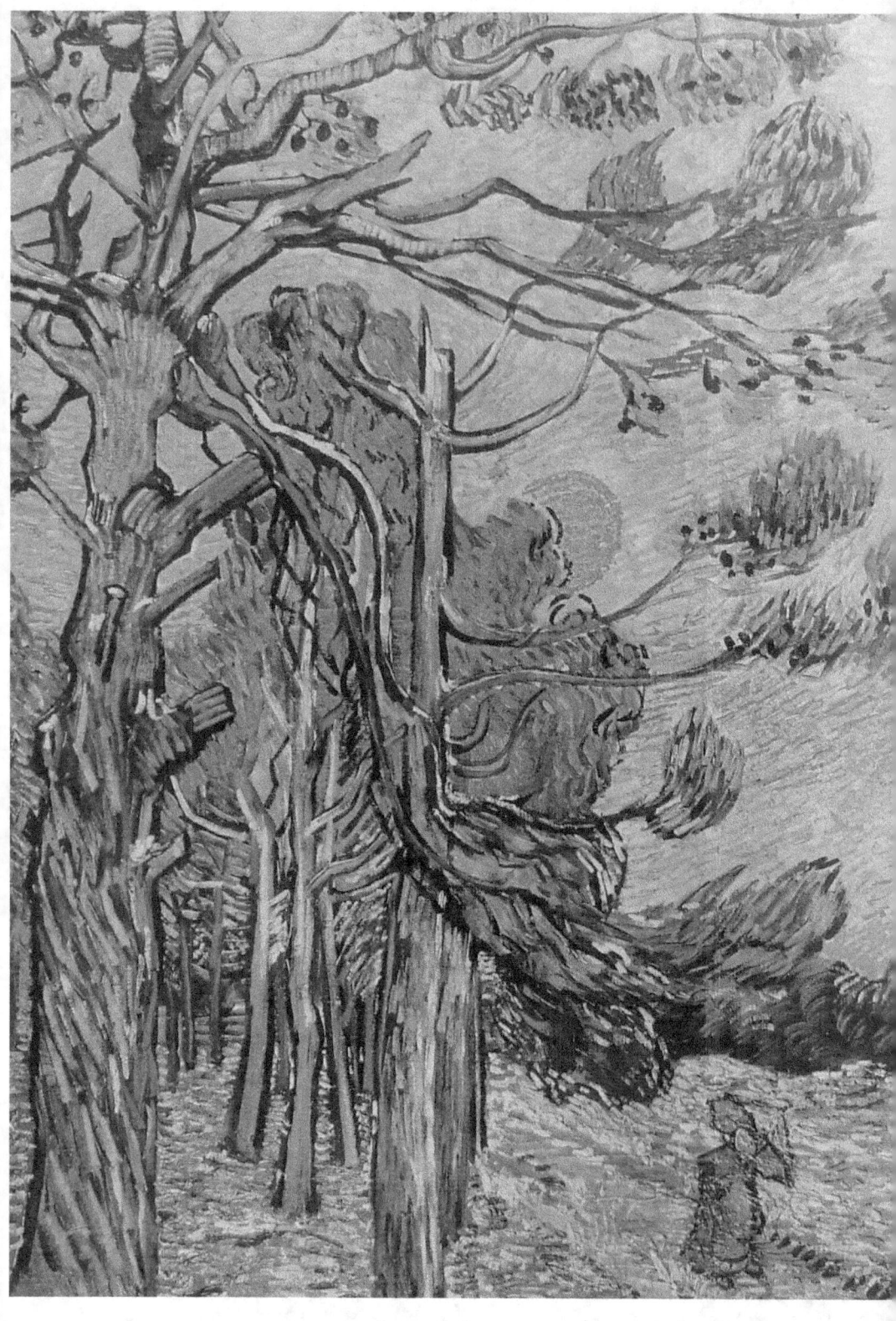

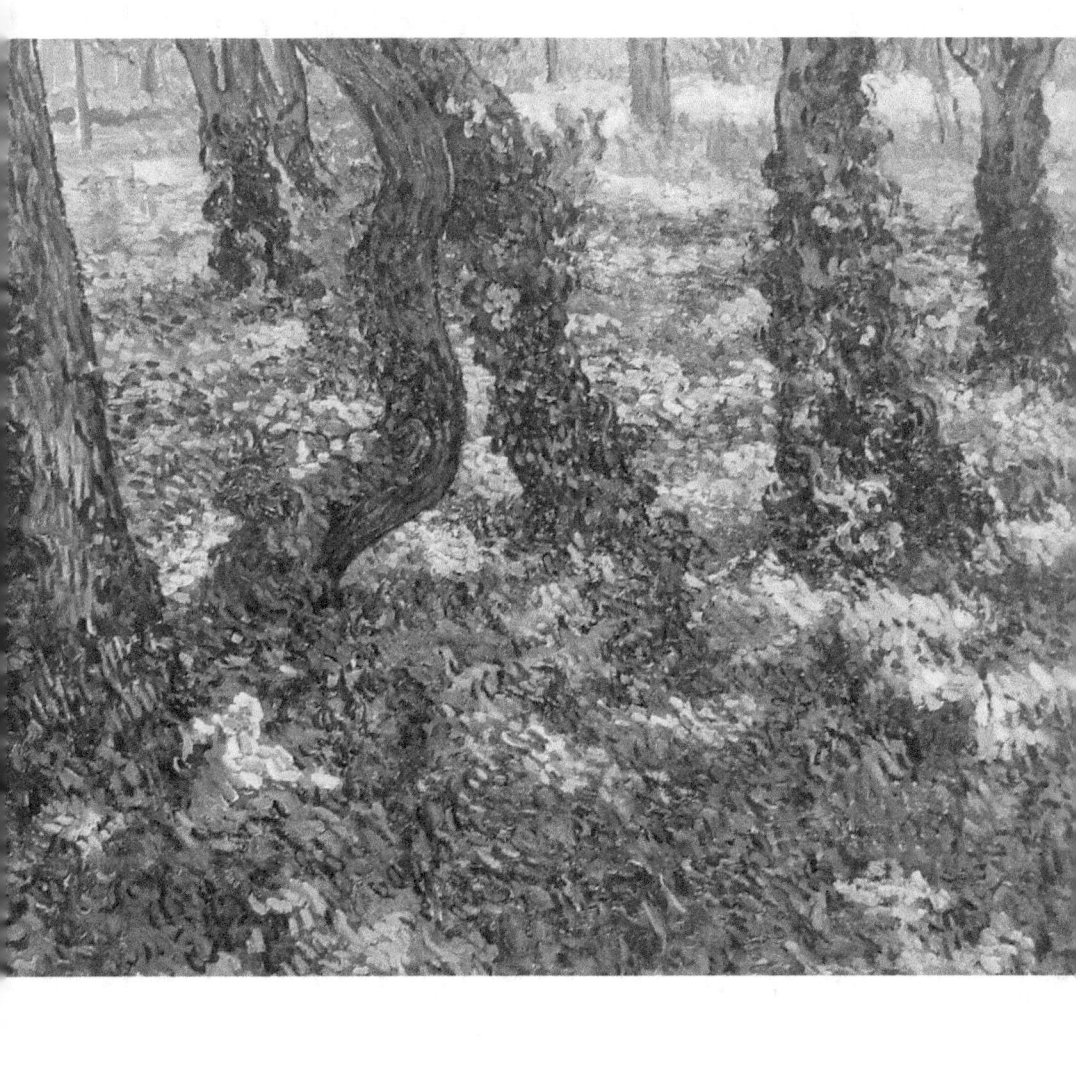

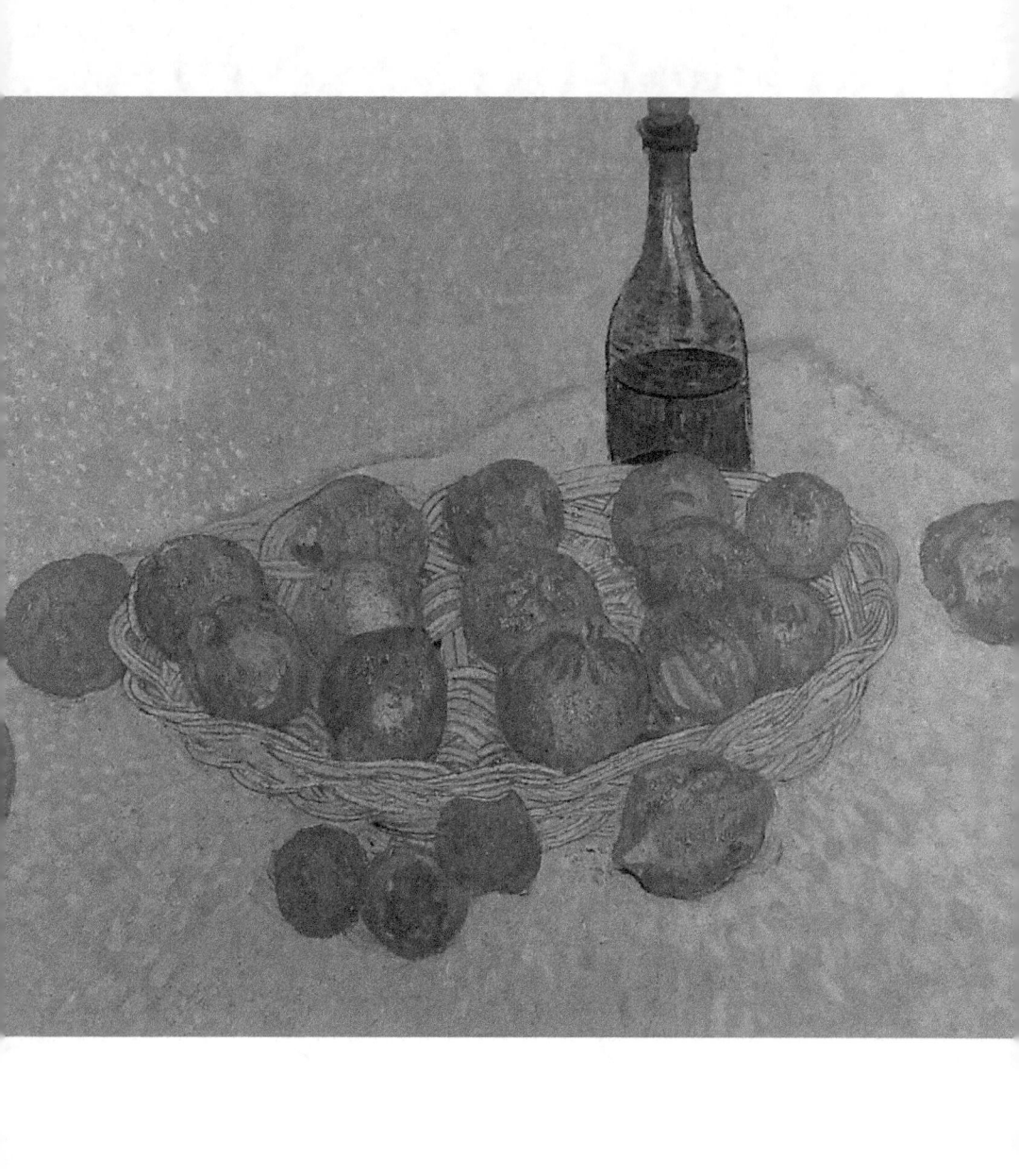

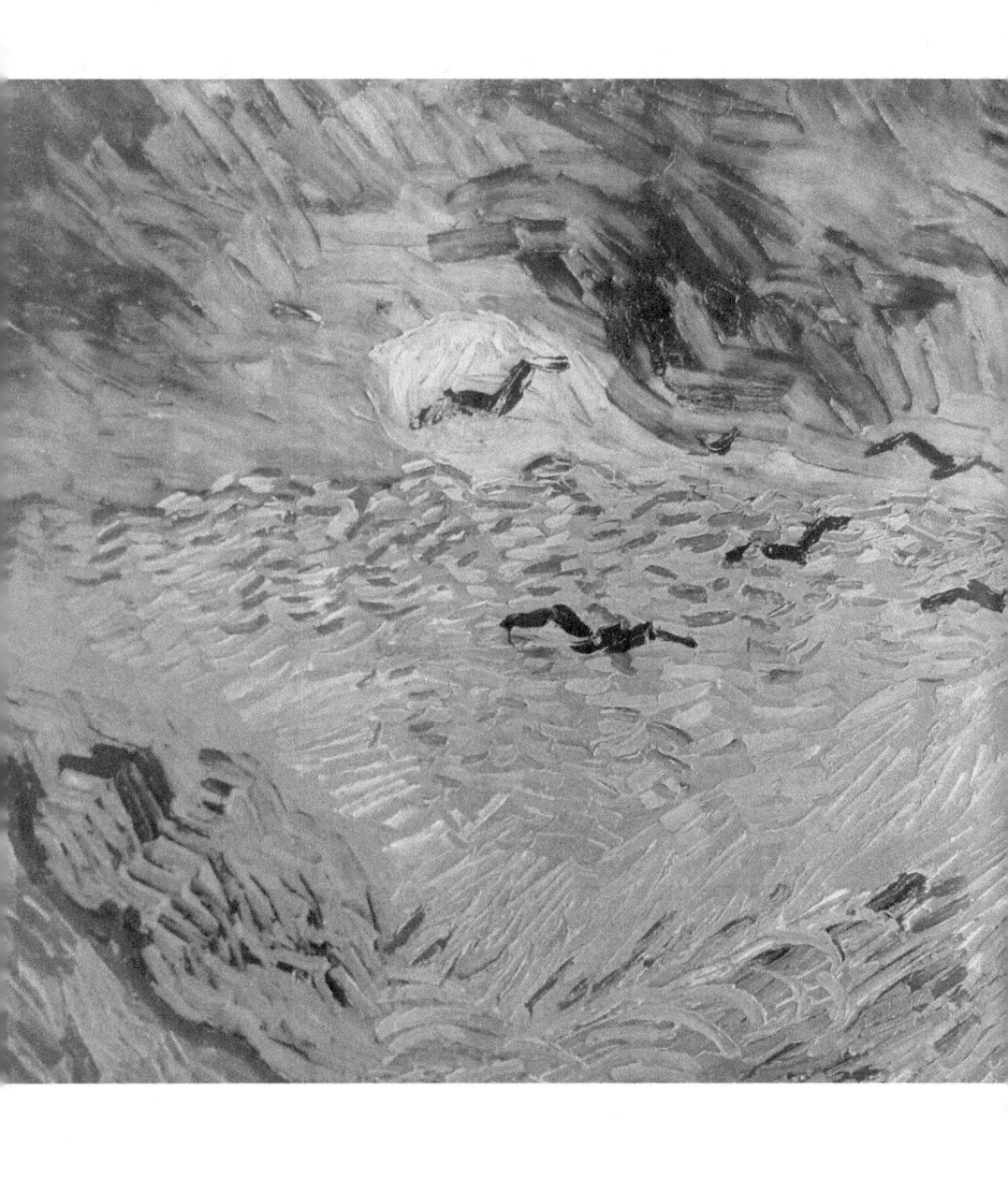

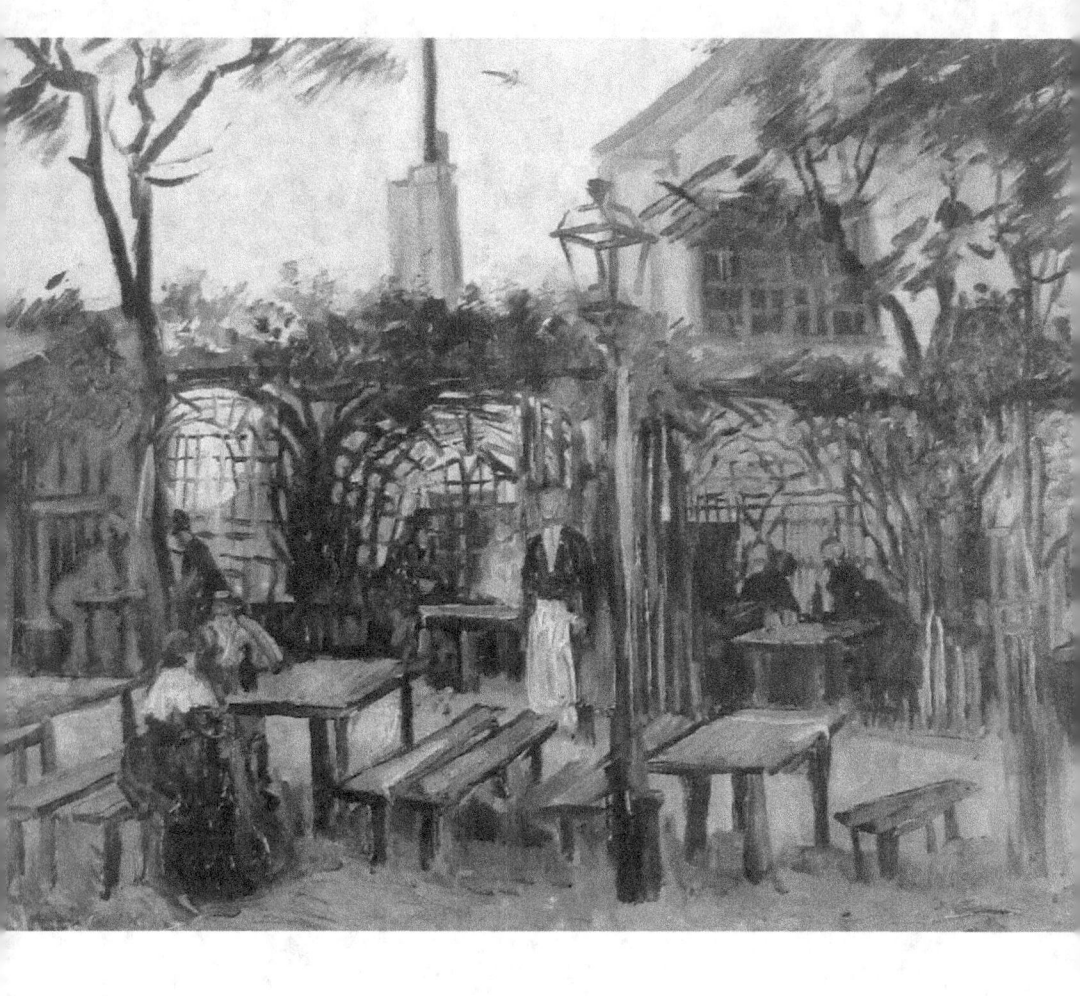

THE ART OF
ANDY GOLDSWORTHY

COMPLETE WORKS: SPECIAL EDITION
(PAPERBACK and HARDBACK)

by William Malpas

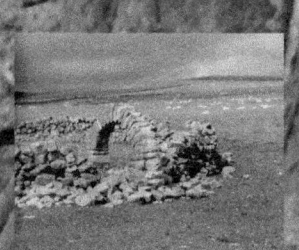
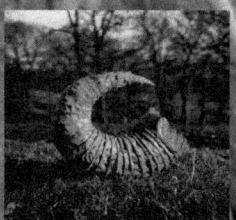

A new, special edition of the study of the contemporary British sculptor, Andy Goldsworthy, including a new introduction, new bibliography and many new illustrations.

This is the most comprehensive, up-to-date, well-researched and in-depth account of Goldsworthy's art available anywhere.

Andy Goldsworthy makes land art. His sculpture is a sensitive, intuitive response to nature, light, time, growth, the seasons and the earth. Goldsworthy's environmental art is becoming ever more popular: 1993's art book *Stone* was a bestseller; the press raved about Goldsworthy taking over a number of London West End art galleries in 1994; during 1995 Goldsworthy designed a set of Royal Mail stamps and had a show at the British Museum. Malpas surveys all of Goldsworthy's art, and analyzes his relation with other land artists such as Robert Smithson, Walter de Maria, Richard Long and David Nash, and his place in the contemporary British art scene.

The Art of Andy Goldsworthy discusses all of Goldsworthy's important and recent exhibitions and books, including the *Sheepfolds* project; the TV documentaries; *Wood* (1996); the New York Holocaust memorial (2003); and Goldsworthy's collaboration on a dance performance.

Illustrations: 70 b/w, 1 colour. 330 pages. New, special, 2nd edition. Publisher: Crescent Moon Publishing. Distributor: Gardners Books.

ISBN 1-86171-059-3 (9781861710598) (Paperback) £25.00 / $44.00

ISBN 1-86171-080-1 (9781861710802) (Hardback) £60.00 / $105.00

ANDY GOLDSWORTHY
IN CLOSE-UP

SPECIAL EDITION (HARDBACK and PAPERBACK)

by William Malpas

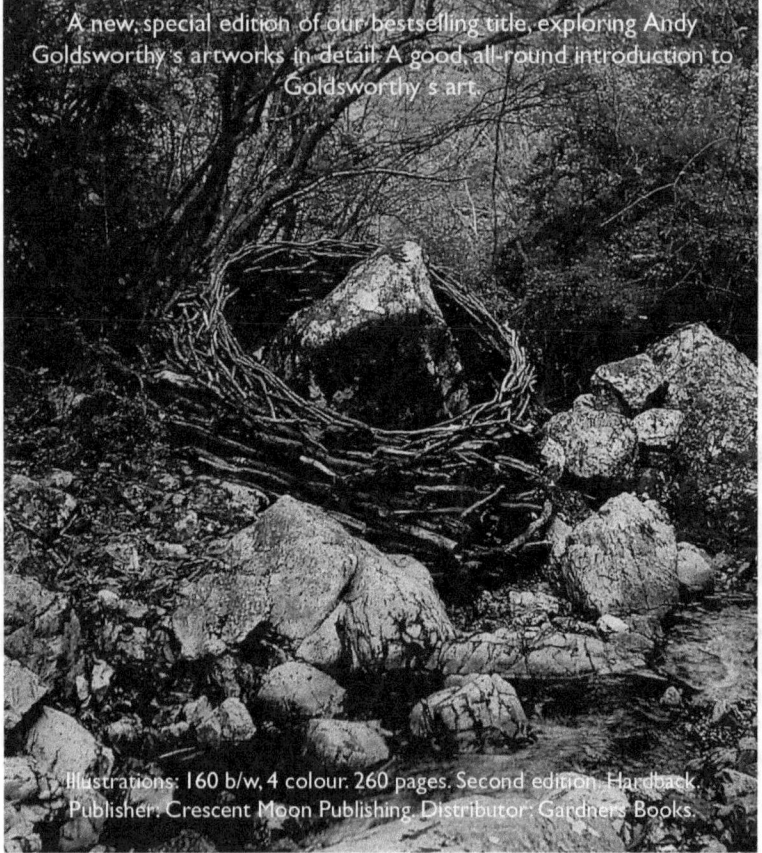

A new, special edition of our bestselling title, exploring Andy Goldsworthy's artworks in detail. A good, all-round introduction to Goldsworthy's art.

Illustrations: 160 b/w, 4 colour. 260 pages. Second edition. Hardback. Publisher: Crescent Moon Publishing. Distributor: Gardners Books.

ISBN 1-86171-094-1 (9781861710949) (Hbk) £60.00 / $105.00

ISBN 1-86171-091-7 (9781861710919) (Pbk) £25.00 / $44.00

Available from bookstores. amazon.com, play.com, tesco.com, and other web-sites.
In the United States from Baker & Taylor, (800) 7753760 or (800) 7751100 or (908) 5417062. electser@btol.com or btinfo@btol.com.

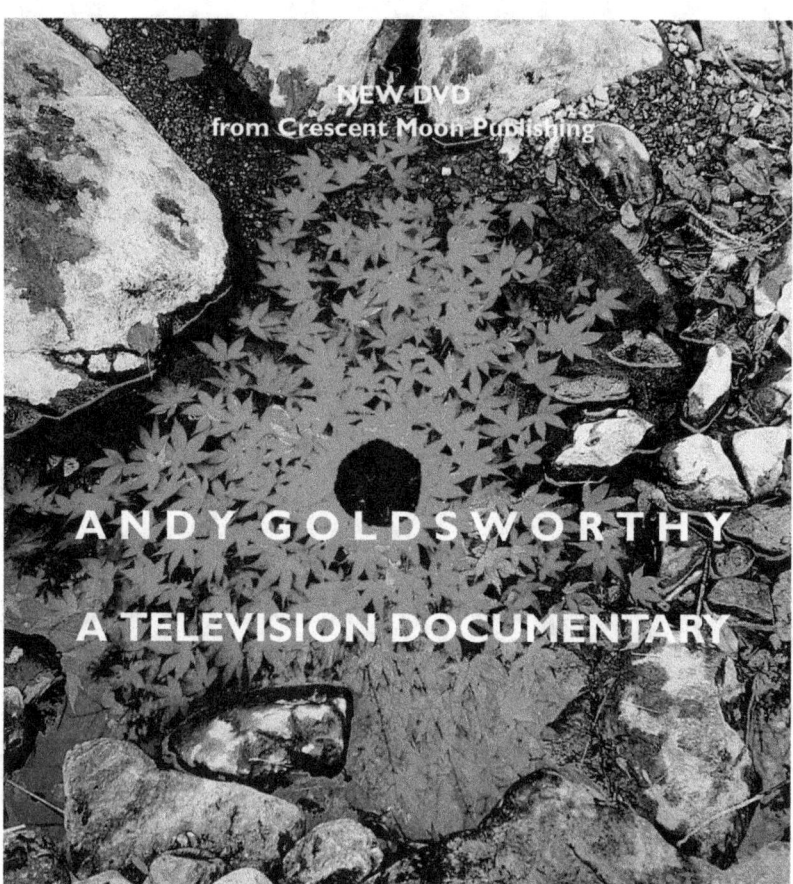

NEW DVD
from Crescent Moon Publishing

ANDY GOLDSWORTHY

A TELEVISION DOCUMENTARY

Andy Goldsworthy makes land art. His sculpture is a sensitive, intuitive response to nature, light, time, growth, the seasons and the earth. Goldsworthy's environmental art is becoming ever more popular: his art books are bestsellers; he has exhibited around the world; important and recent exhibitions include the Sheepfolds project; the Washington installation (2005); Passage (2004); the New York Holocaust memorial (2003); and a collaboration on a dance performance.

This video documentary surveys every aspect of Andy Goldsworthy's art, and all of his major works. It also discusses his relation with other land artists such as Robert Smithson, Walter de Maria, Richard Long and David Nash, and his place in the contemporary art scene in the UK.

This is the only TV documentary of its kind available on DVD and video.

EXTRAS

Resources: further reading; complete bibliography of Andy Goldsworthy, and life and work (on DVD-ROM); and weblinks.
Photo library of land artworks.
Extra footage.

55 minutes. PAL and NTSC. Colour. DVD. Multi-region. VHS video.
Stereo. E (Exempt from classification)

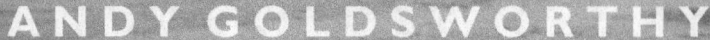

ANDY GOLDSWORTHY

TOUCHING NATURE:
SPECIAL EDITION

(PAPERBACK and HARDBACK)

by William Malpas

A new, special and updated edition of our bestselling title, providing an excellent general introduction to the art of Andy Goldsworthy.

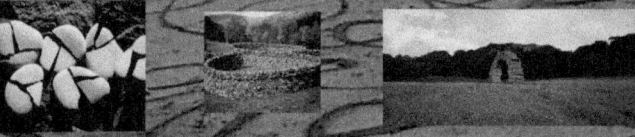

Illustrations: 75 b/w, 2 colour. 354 pages. Third edition. Paperback.

Publisher: Crescent Moon Publishing. Distributor: Gardners Books.

ISBN 1-86171-056-9 (9781861717) (Paperback) £25.00 / $44.00

ISBN 1-86171-087-9 (9781861710871) (Hardback) £60.00 / $105.00

LAND ART

A COMPLETE GUIDE TO LANDSCAPE, ENVIRONMENTAL, EARTHWORKS, NATURE, SCULPTURE AND INSTALLATION ART

by William Malpas

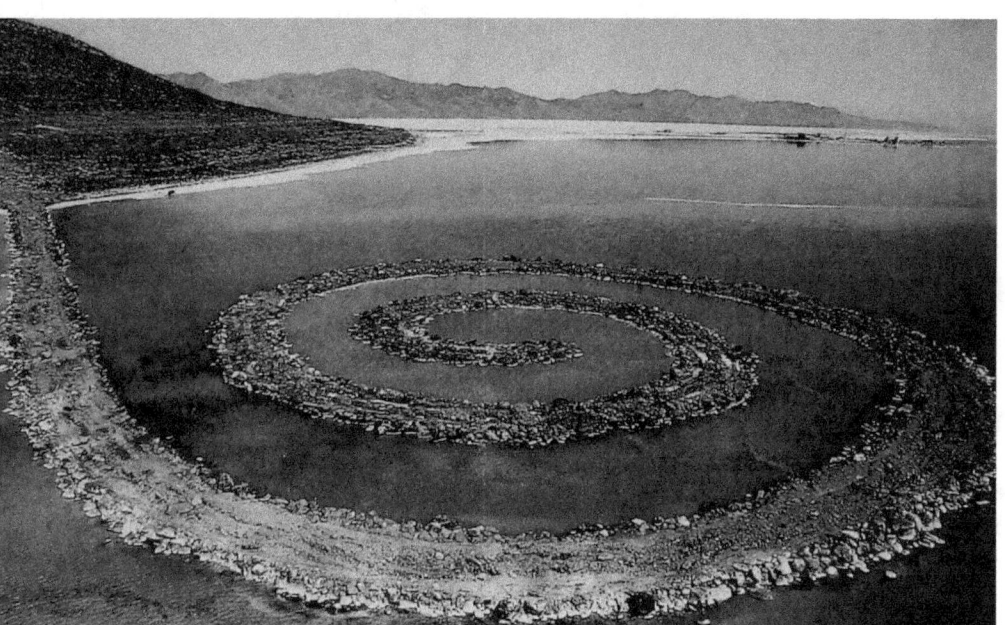

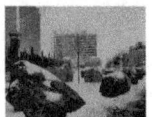 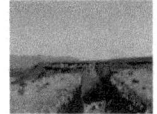 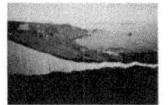 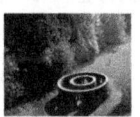 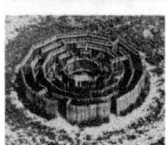

A new, special edition of our popular book on land art.
Chapters on land artists such as Robert Smithson, Walter de Maria, Christo,
Michael Heizer, Richard Long and Andy Goldsworthy.

Illustrations: 35 b/w, 2 colour. 314 pages. First edition. Paperback.

Publisher: Crescent Moon Publishing. Distributor: Gardners Books.

ISBN 1-86171-062-3 (9781861710628) £25.00 / $44.00

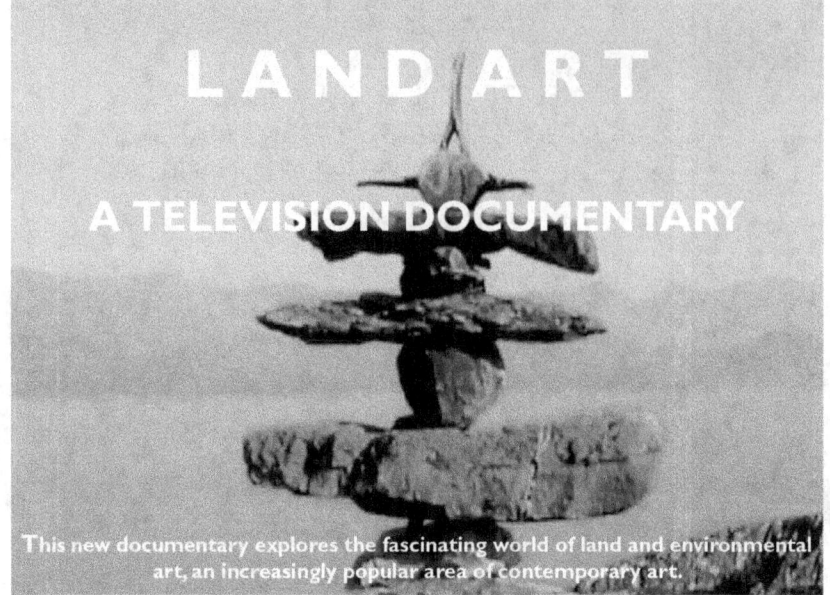

LAND ART IN CLOSE-UP

SPECIAL EDITION (PAPERBACK)

by William Malpas

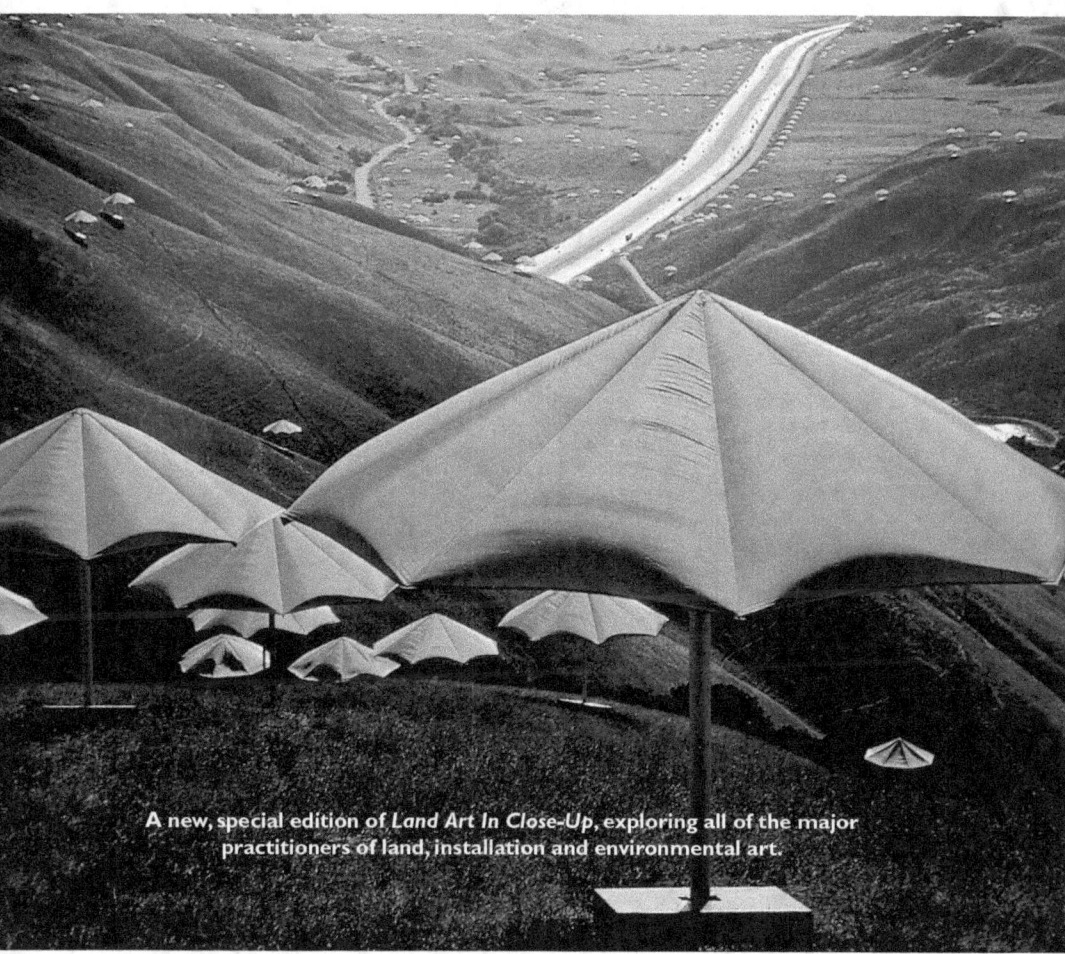

A new, special edition of *Land Art In Close-Up*, exploring all of the major practitioners of land, installation and environmental art.

Illustrations: 161 b/w, 2 colour. 248 pages. Second edition. Paperback.

Publisher: Crescent Moon Publishing. Distributor: Gardners Books.

ISBN 1-86171-092-5 (9781861710925) £25.00 / $44.00

MINIMAL ART AND ARTISTS

FROM THE 1960S AND AFTER

by Laura Garrard

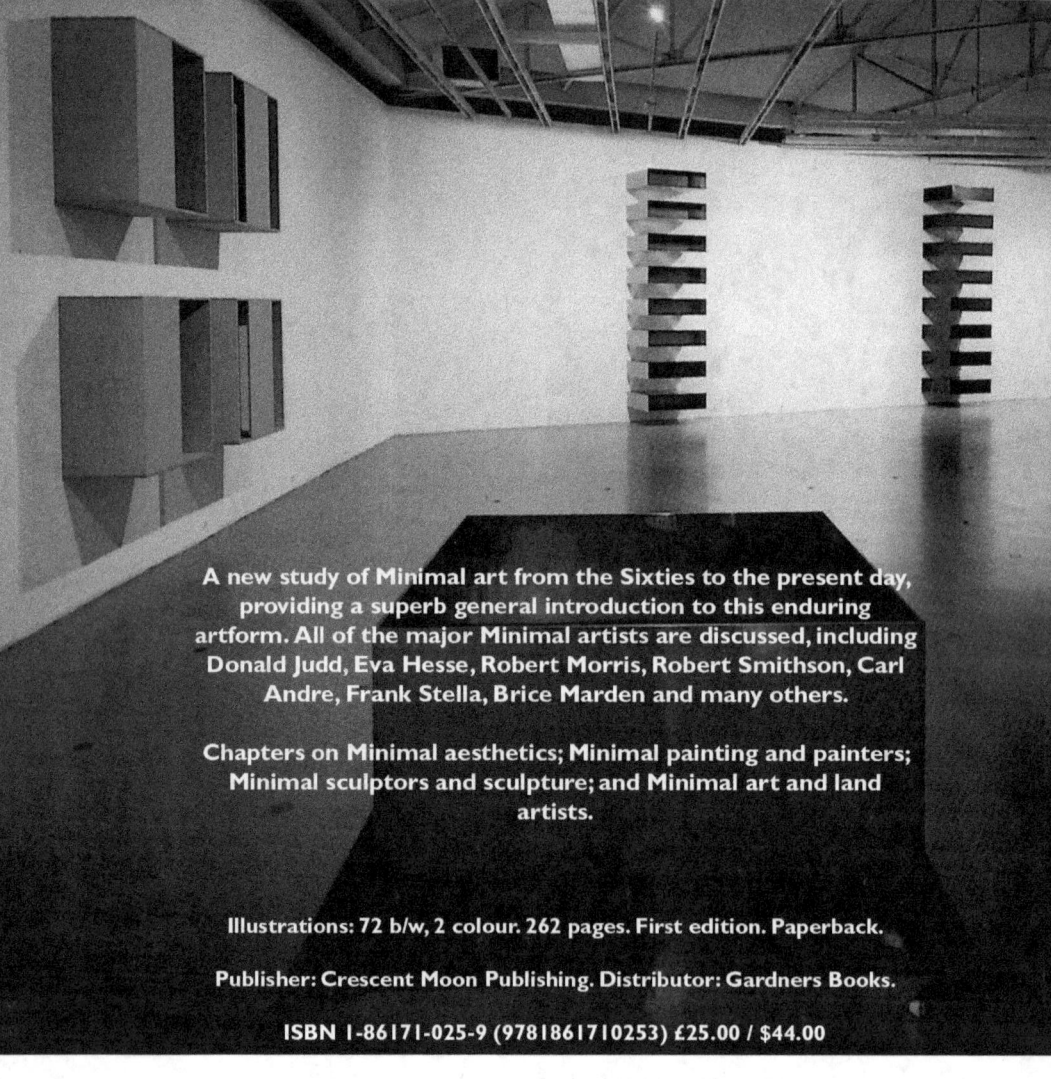

A new study of Minimal art from the Sixties to the present day, providing a superb general introduction to this enduring artform. All of the major Minimal artists are discussed, including Donald Judd, Eva Hesse, Robert Morris, Robert Smithson, Carl Andre, Frank Stella, Brice Marden and many others.

Chapters on Minimal aesthetics; Minimal painting and painters; Minimal sculptors and sculpture; and Minimal art and land artists.

Illustrations: 72 b/w, 2 colour. 262 pages. First edition. Paperback.

Publisher: Crescent Moon Publishing. Distributor: Gardners Books.

ISBN 1-86171-025-9 (9781861710253) £25.00 / $44.00

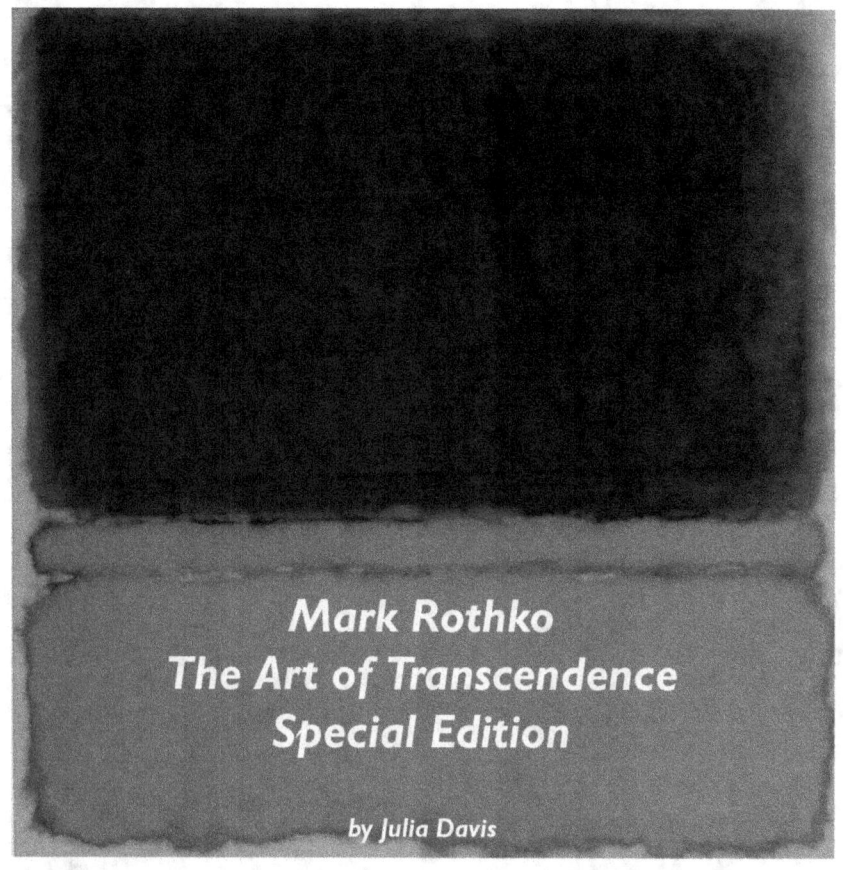

Mark Rothko
The Art of Transcendence
Special Edition

by Julia Davis

Mark Rothko, the American Abstract Expressionist painter, is one of the most widely celebrated of all 20th century artists. His paintings are huge and haunting, marked by themes of tragedy and transcendence. Davis covers Rothko's development from the post-Surrealist semi-figurative works through the radiant canvases of the 1950s, with their floating 'clouds' or 'forms', to the intensity and religiosity of the late mural sequences, the so-called 'Rothko chapels' of Houston, Harvard and the Tate Gallery.

Painters Series   220pp   Bibliography, illustrations, notes   New, 3rd, special edition   ISBN 1-86171-072-0   £14.99 / $26.00

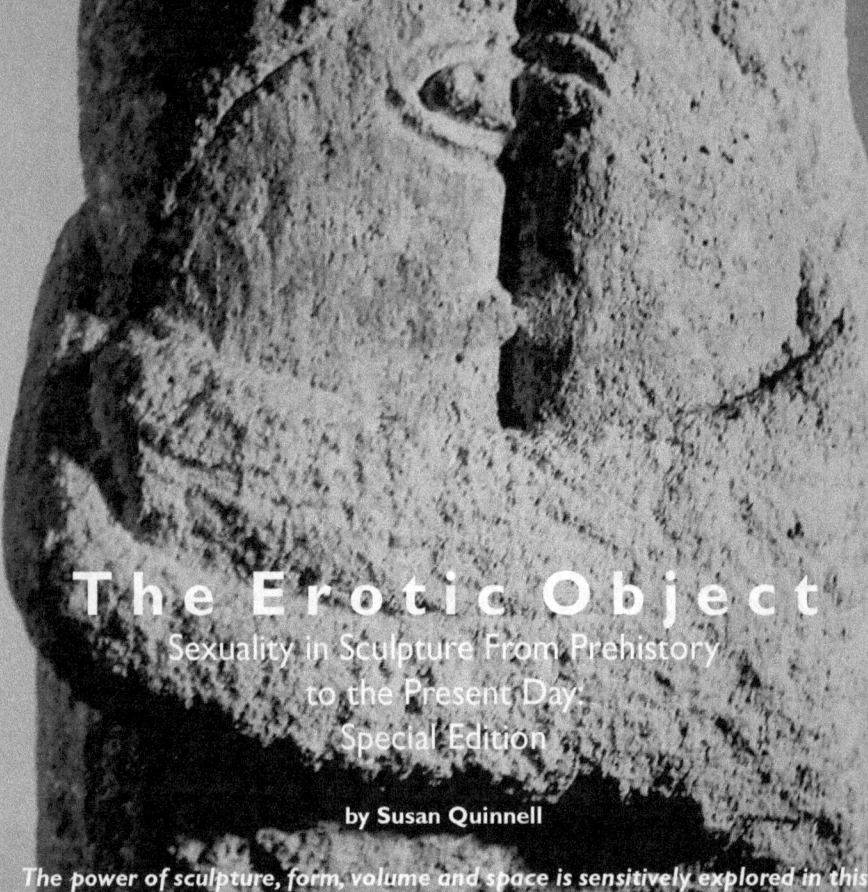

The Erotic Object
Sexuality in Sculpture From Prehistory
to the Present Day:
Special Edition

by Susan Quinnell

The power of sculpture, form, volume and space is sensitively explored in this wide-ranging study. Featuring discussions of many famous sculptors: Michelangelo, Canova, Rodin, Brancusi, Picasso, Hepworth and Bernini. Many contemporary artists are discussed, including installation and performance artists (Catherine Elwes, Karen Finley, Carolee Schneemann), and women sculptors such as Alice Aycock, Mary Miss, Rebecca Horn, Nancy Graves, Eva Hesse, Kathe Kollwitz and Judy Chicago.
A new special edition, with many new illustrations, a new introduction and bibliography.

(Sculptors Series)   Illustrations, bibliography, notes   326pp.   3rd edition
ISBN 1-86171-069-0   £25.00 / $37.50

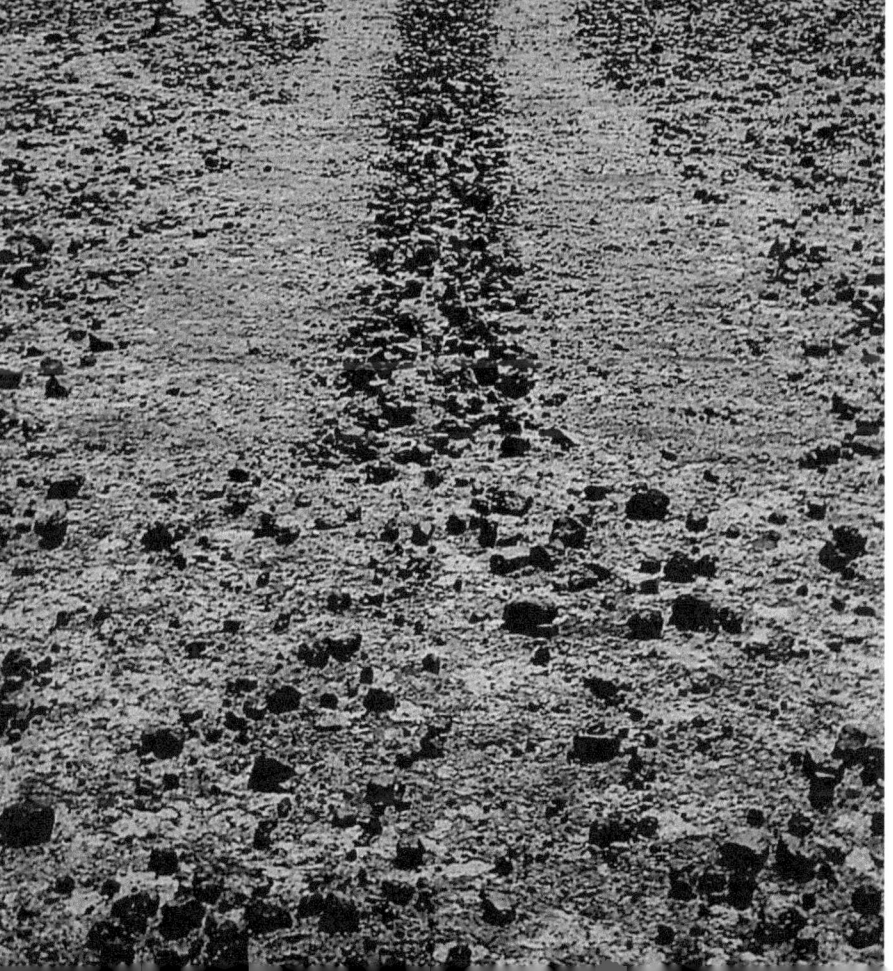

THE ART OF RICHARD LONG

COMPLETE WORKS : SPECIAL EDITION
(HARDBACK and PAPERBACK)

by William Malpas

A new study of the British artist Richard Long, an important contemporary international artist. The most detailed, in-depth exploration of Richard Long's art currently available.

Illustrations: 48 b/w, 2 colour. 439 pages.
First edition. Hardback and paperback editions.

Publisher: Crescent Moon Publishing. Distributor: Gardners Books.

ISBN 1-86171-079-8 (9781861710796) (Hardback) £60.00 / $105.00

ISBN 1-86171-081-X (9781861710819) (Paperback) £25.00 / $44.00

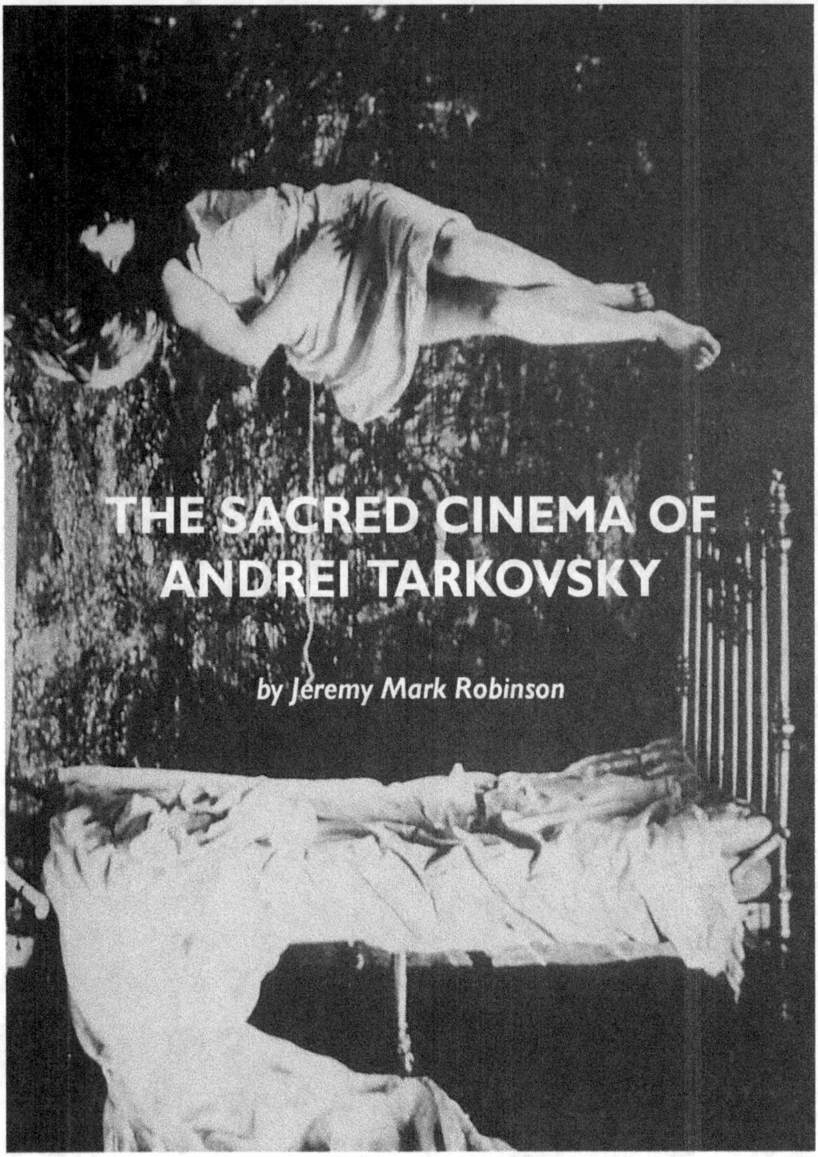

THE SACRED CINEMA OF
ANDREI TARKOVSKY

by Jeremy Mark Robinson

A new study of the Russian filmmaker Andrei Tarkovsky (1932-1986), director of seven feature films, including *Andrei Roublyov, Mirror, Solaris, Stalker* and *The Sacrifice*.

This is one of the most comprehensive and detailed studies of Tarkovsky's cinema available. Every film is explored in depth, with scene-by-scene analyses. All aspects of Tarkovsky's output are critiqued, including editing, camera, staging, script, budget, collaborations, production, sound, music, performance and spirituality. Tarkovsky is placed with a European New Wave tradition of filmmaking, alongside directors like Ingmar Bergman, Carl Theodor Dreyer, Pier Paolo Pasolini and Robert Bresson.

An essential addition to film studies.

Illustrations: 150 b/w, 4 colour. 682 pages. First edition. Hardback.

Publisher: Crescent Moon Publishing. Distributor: Gardners Books.

ISBN 1-86171-096-8 (9781861710963) £60.00 / $105.00

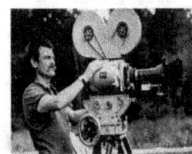